FOLLIES
AND
PLEASURE
PAVILIONS

England

Ireland

Scotland

Wales

HARRY N. ABRAMS, INC.
PUBLISHERS
New York

FOLLIES AND PLEASURE PAVILIONS

England

Ireland

Scotland

Wales

PHOTOGRAPHS BY GEORGE MOTT

Introduction by
Gervase Jackson-Stops
Text by George Mott
and Sally Sample Aall

Editor: Adele Westbrook
Designer: Elissa Ichiyasu

Library of Congress
Cataloging-in-Publication Data
Mott, George.
Follies and pleasure pavilions:
England, Ireland, Scotland, Wales/
photographs by George Mott;
introduction by Gervase Jackson-Stops;
commentary text by George Mott and
Sally Sample Aall.
p.   cm.
Bibliography: p.
Includes index.
ISBN 0–8109–1175–2
1. Pavilions—Great Britain.
2. Follies (Architecture)—Great Britain.
3. Architecture, Domestic—Great Britain.
4. Architecture, Modern—17th-18th
centuries—Great Britain.
5. Architecture, Modern—19th century—
Great Britain.
I. Aall, Sally Sample, 1926–
II. Title.
NA8450.M68 1989
728'.9—dc19   88–7463

CONTENTS

INTRODUCTION

Follies and eye-catchers, gazebos and belvederes, temples and pagodas, dairies and bath houses, menageries and aviaries, sham castles and artificial ruins—there is scarcely a country house in England, Ireland, Scotland, or Wales that does not have its quota of garden buildings. Crowning a windy hilltop or reflected in the calm waters of a serpentine lake, windowpanes glinting in the last rays of the evening sun or pinnacles and battlements looming up through a Scotch mist, they have a magic, even in decay, that never fails to enchant.

What is it that gives these buildings their particular excitement? Why does the pulse quicken as a distant tower comes into view at the end of an avenue, or a winding woodland path suddenly breaks into a clearing to reveal a pyramid, a grotto, or a long-forgotten bath house? Surprise has always been central to the idea of the folly: what you find may be Classical or Gothic, Chinese or Egyptian; made of tree roots or tufa, shells or bones; a monument to a wife or a horse; a place for keeping tigers or chickens. Legends cluster around such buildings, and their very names intrigue: the Treacle Eater at Barwick Park, the Needle's Eye at Wentworth Woodhouse, the Jealous Wall at Belvedere in Westmeath, the Whim at Blair Atholl.

If there is a common link among them it is, in fact, the element of fantasy, for whereas the design of the country house had to conform to a conventional life-style, and cope with the practicalities of everyday existence, the plans for a garden building could afford to be more experimental and imaginative. It is no accident that Gibbs's Gothick Temple at Stowe (1741–44) is among the earliest monuments of the Gothic Revival in England, nor that James "Athenian" Stuart's Temple of Theseus at Hagley, designed in 1758, may claim to be the first Neoclassical building north of the Alps.

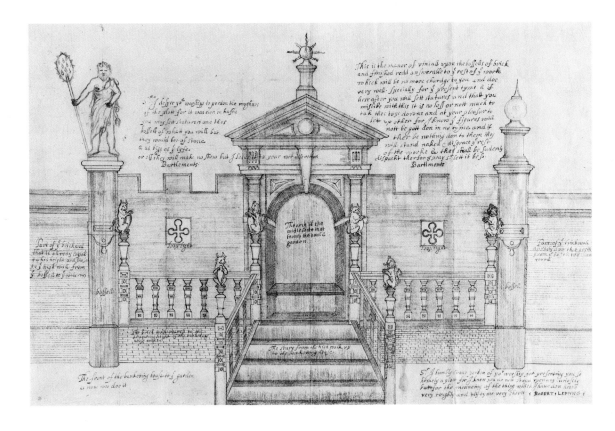

1 • Design for a banqueting house at Blickling Hall, Norfolk, England, by Robert Lyminge, c.1625. The National Trust, London

2 • Landscape near Rome with a View of the Ponte Molle, *by Claude Lorrain. This is the kind of pastoral scene with buildings that lay at the root of the "Picturesque" style in English gardening. Birmingham City Museum and Art Gallery, England*

The idea of the pavilion as an essential adjunct of the pleasure garden dates back to the worlds of ancient Greece and Rome. The younger Pliny's Laurentian Villa had not only a scattering of open and closed porticoes terminating different walks, but also a tower overlooking the entire layout—while at Tivoli, the Emperor Hadrian apparently aimed to reproduce the buildings and sites that he had visited in the course of his travels, including the Stoa Poikile of Athens and the Temple of Serapis near Alexandria. During the Italian Renaissance, these principles were revived (again at Tivoli) in the famous gardens laid out for Cardinal Ippolito d'Este, where the *Rometta* portrayed the Seven Hills of Rome in miniature, together with their major monuments, such as the Colosseum, the Septizonium, and the Pantheon.

3 • The Temple of Bacchus at Painshill, *Surrey, England, attributed to William Hannan, c.1765. Probably designed by Robert Adam, the temple was built of wood, plaster, and papier-mâché. Private Collection*

In Elizabethan England, garden buildings were generally banqueting houses, used in summer for the different dessert courses that followed the main repast—in the same way as the towers that crown the roofs of such buildings as Longleat and Hardwick. Not far enough away from the house to be of a wholly different character, they often, indeed, took the shape of lanterns or cupolas—like the octagonal pavilion at Melford Hall *(colorplate 80)*, or the fanciful, ogee-roofed pavilions flanking the forecourt at Montacute House *(colorplate 83)*. However, the elaborate stage sets built for masques during the Jacobean period by Inigo Jones and his contemporaries, also had an influence on the form of such buildings. The banqueting house like a mock-fort (complete with loopholes and machicolations) that Robert Lyminge designed for the garden at Blickling *(figure 1)*, is a remarkably early example of nostalgia for the Middle Ages—using some of the same motifs as the bridge across the moat on the south front.

Outside the garden proper, in the parks and hunting grounds that surrounded their great houses, the courtiers of Elizabeth I and James I also erected "stands," where spectators could watch the progress of the hunt, and at the same time enjoy the distant prospect of the countryside. The tall Hunting Tower at

Chatsworth, perched on the hillside above the house, is the ancestor of countless eighteenth-century belvederes and prospect towers, with an elaborate series of rooms for entertainment and recreation, involving a day-long expedition from the main house. Smaller stands, with twin cupolas on either side of a viewing platform, can be found at Methley in Yorkshire and at Swarkeston in Derbyshire *(colorplate 114)*, overlooking walled enclosures where more formal equestrian events or coursing competitions might take place.

Tree houses, now only considered suitable sport for children, enjoyed a considerable vogue during the sixteenth and seventeenth centuries, and John Parkinson describes a large lime tree at Cobham in 1629, with its branches trained to form three arbors, one above the other, in each of which "might bee placed halfe an hundred men at the least." One that still exists in an ancient tree at Pitchford in Shropshire *(colorplates 92, 93, 94)*, has a room decorated with pretty Rococo plasterwork, but has a much earlier, half-timbered construction—the forerunner of those later garden buildings that aimed to mimic the work of nature rather than of man: bark houses, shell grottoes, and arbors made of rough-hewn tree trunks.

The neat formal gardens of the Baroque period, based upon French and Dutch prototypes, generally placed more emphasis on canals, parterres, and axial vistas than on garden buildings. But there are exceptions, such as Thomas Archer's Cascade House at Chatsworth, and his magnificent domed Pavilion at Wrest *(colorplates 137, 138)*, which look to Italy for their inspiration, and summon up the world of Isola Bella and

the Villa Lante. The passion for growing exotic fruits, from oranges and lemons to pineapples and pomegranates, also made the "greenhouse" or orangery an inevitable ingredient of the country-house garden. From being a mere "tabernacle of boards," it grew in architectural pretension, reaching heights in William Talman's building at Dyrham, based on Hardouin-Mansart's *orangerie* at Versailles, in Nicholas Hawksmoor's monumental example at Kensington Palace, and—largest of all—the one at Margam in West Glamorgan *(colorplates 75, 76)*, said to contain trees from a sixteenth-century Spanish shipwreck.

The advent of the landscape garden, and the development of theories of the "Picturesque," gave garden buildings a new importance in the early eighteenth century, however, particularly in England. One of the early pioneers of this style was Sir John Vanbrugh, who tried his best to save the ruins of old Woodstock Manor in the park at Blenheim, for its historical associations, and whose massive curtain-walls and bastions on the approach to Castle Howard already show a romantic feeling for the Middle Ages. Claude Lorrain's favorite convention of contrasting a round building with a square one, linked by a bridge in the valley between *(figure 2)*, can also be found in Vanbrugh's juxtaposition of the square Temple of the Winds at Castle Howard *(colorplate 26)* with the Palladian bridge, and the circular Mausoleum beyond *(colorplate 27)*, finally built by

Hawksmoor. Indeed, there is reason to think that Vanbrugh may have planned the pyramid not far away as a tribute to the civilization of Egypt, just as the other buildings represented Greece, Rome, and the Italian Renaissance— a historical progression leading up to Lord Carlisle's own great "temple of the arts," a symbol of a new and still greater age of enlightenment.

The idea of reproducing the classical temples of antiquity, whether in the lush green parkland of domestic Middlesex *(colorplate 91)*, or on the windswept cliff tops of Northern Ireland *(colorplate 36)*, may not always have been so didactic in intention. But it gave architects the opportunity to imitate Roman and Greek models with far greater fidelity than was possible in the design of the country house itself *(figure 3)*. Conceived in the round, these miniature versions of the Athenian acropolis or the Roman forum could also act as multiple view

points—a domed rotunda such as Vanbrugh's at Stowe *(figure 4)* could be placed at the center of a whole system of radiating walks, or a series of temples could be linked by different vistas, as in William Kent's layout at Rousham. Philip Yorke's account of a visit to Studley Royal in 1744 particularly praises the way in which "the same object, taken at a different point of view, is surprisingly diversified and has all the grace of novelty."

4 • *The Rotunda at Stowe, Buckinghamshire, England, designed by Vanbrugh. From an engraving by Rigaud and Baron, dated 1739. The Governors of Stowe School, England*

5 • The Drake-Brockman Family in the
Rotunda at Beachborough House, *Kent,
England, by Edward Haytley, 1743.*
Victoria Art Gallery, Melbourne, Australia

It was Kent who, above all, formulated the ideal of the picturesque garden as a circuit walk, with buildings, statues, cascades, and other "incidents" gradually revealing themselves to the spectator at different angles and in different combinations. As Horace Walpole put it, "where objects were wanting to animate his horizon, his taste as an architect could bestow immediate termination. His buildings, his seats, his temples, were more the work of his pencil than of his compasses. We owe the restoration of Greece and the diffusion of architecture to his skill in landscape."

Kent's close association with the poet Alexander Pope helped give his buildings a literary slant that was also at the core of the "Picturesque" movement. His illustrations for James Thomson's famous poem, *The Seasons* (1730), show many of the elements of his documented garden designs *(figure 6)*, and the whole concept of the Elysian Fields (which he created at Stowe) goes back to Virgil's visions of Arcadia. While Chaucer and Shakespeare took their place here beside Pope in the Temple of British Worthies, it was the classical authors and their treatment of mythology that particularly appealed to landscape gardeners in the mid-eighteenth century. On the most famous of all the circuit walks, at Stourhead *(figure 7)*, the visitor discovers a Virgilian landscape, based upon Lorrain's famous *Landscape with Aeneas at Delos,* now in the National Gallery in London *(figure 9)*. Moreover, the four principal "incidents" on the tour are the Temple of Apollo *(colorplate 107)*, dedicated to the Sun, whose rays give life to the surrounding verdure *(figure*

8*)*; the Pantheon *(colorplate 106)*, dedicated to Hercules, the man-god by whose labors the gardens were made; the Grotto *(colorplate 105)*, ruled over by Neptune, who causes the waters to flow and the lakes to fill; and finally, the Temple of Flora, goddess of spring, at whose behest the flowers grow. Associations of this kind, which would readily have sprung to the minds of Georgian cognoscenti familiar with the classics, were a way of provoking thoughts about nature, and the way in which human beings should respond to it. Even a privy in a dark corner of the gardens at Wrest could be christened the Temple of Cloacina, in tribute to the goddess of sewers.

Books not only provided the sources for such man-made landscapes, they could also furnish it in a more literal way. As early as 1718, Stephen Switzer describes the Wilderness at Dyrham with a central garden "round an aspiring Fir-Tree . . . from whence your Prospect terminates in a large old Church, at a very great distance. I never in my whole Life did see so agreeable a Place for the sublimest Studies, as this is in the summer, and here are small Desks erected in Seats for that Purpose." Kent's design for Merlin's Cave in Richmond Park, done in 1735, shows the interior as a comfortable subterranean library, while Dr. Richard Pococke, visiting Wimborne St. Giles in 1754, admired "a round pavilion on a Mount, Shake Spears house, in which is a small statue of him & his works in a Glass case; & in all the houses & seats are books in hanging Glass cases." David Garrick had a similar temple dedicated to Shakespeare on the banks of the Thames at Twickenham *(colorplate 52)*, but it would be difficult to imagine a better setting for the "sublimest Studies"

6 • One of William Kent's illustrations for James Thomson's The Seasons, *published in 1730. J. B. Morrell Library, University of York, England*

than the Earl-Bishop of Bristol's library in the Mussenden Temple at Downhill *(colorplate 36)*, with only the surf beating on the rocks below for company.

In addition to literary and pictorial associations, garden buildings could have historical, political, or even erotic overtones. Nowhere were the political messages clearer than at Stowe, where the Temples, putting into practice their family motto: *Templa Quam Dilecta* ("How Beautiful are Thy Temples"), erected a whole series of garden buildings almost as propaganda for their parliamentary faction of patriotic Whigs. Thus the Temple of Ancient Virtue, containing statues of great commanders of the Roman Empire, was contrasted with the ruined Temple of Modern Virtue, a reflection on the corrupt members of Walpole's administration. At the same time, Gibbs's Gothick Temple, surrounded by Rysbrack's statues of the Saxon deities who gave their names to the days of the week, was intended to recall the ancient native liberties of the English under the Druids—a tradition shared with the Hanoverian kings, in opposition to the autocracy of Carolingian France.

In this context, King Alfred also became something of a cult hero, as the lawgiver who enshrined the rights of the individual in his constitution. A leading figure in the Temple of Brit-ish Worthies at Stowe, Alfred was also commemorated by a great tower at Stourhead *(colorplate 109)*, built on the spot where he was said to have raised his standard before fighting the Danes. Another popular legend was that of Robin Hood, the scourge of Sherwood Forest in Nottingham-shire, who was seen not as a bandit, but as a champion of the populace against the Norman oppressor. Various rustic huts called after him survive, but also an ambitious por-ticoed temple as far afield as Halswell in Somerset.

Modern history could equally provide the inspiration for a folly, more often than not representing the viewpoint of a minority, determined to have its say. Sir Thomas Tresham's Triangular Lodge at Rushton *(colorplates 99, 100, 101)*, was not simply a pun on the first three letters of his name, but an open advertisement of his Roman Catholicism with its references to the Trinity—at a time when recusants were punished by the imposition of heavy fines. In the same way, Sir Thomas Gascoigne's Triumphant Arch at Parlington cannot have made him very popular in Yorkshire, with its boldly lettered inscription: "LIBERTY. IN. N. AMERICA. TRIUMPHANT. MDCCLXXXIII."

9 • Landscape with Aeneas at Delos, *by Claude Lorrain, 1672. National Gallery, London*

No style had greater associational value on literary or historical grounds than the "Gothick," as it was commonly spelled in the eighteenth century—and as it has subsequently been used to differentiate the whimsical (and often pasteboard) manner of the Georgians *(figure 10)*, from the more scholarly (and often soulless) reconstructions of the later Gothic Revival. According to the English translation of Roger de Piles's *Cours de Peinture*, published in 1743, "buildings in general are a great ornament in landskip, even when they are *Gothick*, or appear partly inhabited, and partly ruinous: they raise the imagination by the use they are thought to be designed for; as appears from antient towers, which seem to have been the habitations of fairies, and are now retreats for shepherds and owls."

There may have been an element of snobbery in the great popularity of Gothick garden buildings toward the middle of the eighteenth century. For whereas an ambitious Whig land-owner might wish to replace his ancestors' old manor with a new house in the fashionable Palladian style, he would not wish to be mistaken for a parvenu. The ruins of an old castle within the grounds would not only be a picturesque incident on the circuit walk, but would also suggest the ancient lineage of his family—perhaps even its descent from a signatory of the Magna Carta. It was in this spirit that Horace Walpole praised the castle at Hagley, designed by Sanderson Miller in 1749, as having "the true rust of the Barons' War." At Wimpole, Miller's

rather similar castle (placed on a hillside on axis with the house), was built for the Hardwickes, who had acquired the estate only a few years before, and were still keener to evoke a distinguished past. A verse printed under an engraving of the castle made in 1777 *(figure 11)*, shows just the kind of images such a building could conjure up in the eighteenth-century mind:

When Henry stemmed Ierne's story
    flood,
And bowed to Britain's yoke her stormy
    brood,
When by true courage and false Zeal
    impelled
Richard encamp'd on Salem's palmy
    field,
On towers like these Earl, Baron,
    Vavasor
Hung high their floating banners on
    the air.

The engraving of the castle at Wimpole was accompanied by another, showing James "Athenian" Stuart's temple *(figure 12)*, as an intentional contrast between ancient and modern architecture—and as the century progressed, the idea of the park as an extended "cabinet of curiosities," or a kind of open-air museum of architecture, became more common. Chinese pagodas, Turkish tents, Egyptian pyramids, Indian gate lodges, were conceived almost as a guide to previous civilizations, extending Vanbrugh's earlier progression at Castle Howard.

The taste for the exotic accounted for a particular fascination with chinoiserie, long popular in the shape of lacquer, porcelain, and silks imported through the English and Dutch East India Companies, but rarely given architectural form before the building of the Chinese House at Shugborough in 1747 *(figure 13)*. Admiral Lord Anson, whose elder brother Thomas lived at Shugborough, had called at Canton during his circumnavigation of 1740–44, and the pavilion built to contain much of the porcelain and other objects he had collected there, was said to be "a true pattern of the Architecture of that Nation, taken in the country by the skilful pencil of Sir Percy Brett" (one of his companions). Still more accurate were the *Designs of Chinese Buildings*, published by Sir William Chambers in 1757, the fruit of his own experience as a youth on board a Swedish merchant ship. Chambers's pagoda at Kew, 163 feet high (and built four years later), is one of the most ambitious of all eighteenth-century garden buildings—it inspired a rash of tea-houses, boat-houses, dairies *(colorplates 133, 134)*, and "fretwork" arbors *à la chinoise* in the years that followed.

Chambers also drew attention to the way in which the Chinese "contrive different scenes for morning, noon, and evening; erecting, at the proper points of view, buildings adapted to the recreations of each particular time of day." Much thought was similarly given to the placing of English garden buildings and their uses, occasionally adapted to nocturnal as well as to daytime pursuits. The charming shell grotto that the 2nd Earl of Halifax built for his mistress in the garden of her house at Hampton Court, has alcoves representing Dusk on the west side and Dawn on the east, each of which was

12 • The Park Building at Wimpole, designed by James "Athenian" Stuart. From an engraving of 1777. The National Trust, London.

equipped with a couch and a miniature fireplace—while much use was made of stalagmites and giant cowrie shells, for their almost too obvious male and female symbolism.

Sir Francis Dashwood went still further with his Temple of Venus at West Wycombe, built on a mount with curving wing walls supposed to represent a pair of legs, flanking the oval opening to a cave. The series of caves that he excavated in the hill below the parish church were also the setting for meetings of the Hell Fire Club, whose members and their lady friends are said to have dressed frequently as monks and nuns. Such

junketings are reminiscent of Francis Coventry's article in *The World*, published in 1753, describing the house and garden laid out by Squire Mushroom: "as every folly must have a name, the squire informs you that *by way of whim* he has christened this place *little Marybon;* at the upper end of which you are conducted into a pompous, clumsy and gilded building, said to be a temple, and consecrated to Venus; for no other reason which I could learn, but because the squire riots here sometimes in vulgar love with a couple of the orange-wenches, taken from the purlieus of the playhouse."

The exotic and the erotic may sometimes have gone hand in hand, but on the whole there was a more serious spirit of inquiry behind the different styles of garden building

and their decoration. Shells and minerals (or "petrifications") were in particular studied with scientific intensity, and the number of books on these subjects in country-house libraries suggests how carefully collections were formed and arranged. Families with naval traditions, or with financial interests in shipping and overseas trade, had especially good opportunities here, and it is significant that one of the finest shell grottoes in England was made for a Bristol merchant, Thomas Goldney, at Clifton. Sometimes the decoration was carried out by amateurs, such as the Duchess of Richmond and her daughters, whose initials appear in the ceiling of the grotto at Goodwood; but more often

it was the work of professionals such as Josiah Lane of Tisbury, who decorated Fonthill, Oatlands, and Painshill, or John Castles of Marylebone, recorded by Pococke as being responsible for the spectacular example at Wimborne St. Giles, now in a sad state of decay. The grotto in Pope's garden at Twickenham is another example of the scientific character of such buildings, for the Swedish minister Gyllenborg writes in 1725 of the doors being shut, and the room becoming "on the instant a *camera obscura*, on the walls of which all the objects of the river, hills, woods, and boats are forming a moving picture in their visible radiations."

The word "folly" is often used to imply a building that is useless, whimsical, or inconsequential. Certain "eye-catchers," such as Kent's strange arched screen at Rousham *(figure 15)*, way outside the park and intended to make a bold silhouette at a distance, certainly fall into this category. But the large majority of English garden buildings are functional, even multipurpose. Robert Adam's fishing pavilion at Kedleston *(colorplates 71, 72, 73, 74)*, combines a cold plunge bath in the center, fed by a spring immediately behind, two boathouses flanking it, and a fishing room with a large Venetian window above, enabling the ladies of the house to cast a line straight into the water without having to subject themselves to the rays of the sun. James Paine's Temple of Diana at Weston Park *(colorplates 123, 124, 125)*, was used as an orangery, dairy, teahouse, and music room; while the Duke of Hamilton's palatial "dog kennels" at Chatelherault *(colorplate 28)* served as quarters for the hunt servants, with private family quarters for eating and sleeping (adjoining the walled flower garden), and a grandstand for watching the races held in the park below.

14 • A design for a Chinese pavilion at Wallington, Northumberland, England, dated 1752. The National Trust, London

15 • The Temple of the Mill and Eye-Catcher at Rousham, Oxfordshire, England. From a watercolor by William Kent, c.1738–41. C. Cottrell-Dormer, Esq.

16 • *The lake and cascade at West Wycombe Park, Buckinghamshire, England. From an engraving after William Hannan, 1752. The National Trust, London*

Many pavilions neighboring lakes incorporated icehouses: often beautifully constructed spherical chambers of brick, that would be filled in the winter with huge blocks of ice, using special horse-drawn cutters. Not only were they used to cool wines and to store other delicacies in the summer, but also to refrigerate whole sides of beef and venison that had to be kept for any length of time.

Lake pavilions often took the form of miniature forts, and this too was also functional, since mock naval engagements were a favorite pastime.
At Newstead Abbey, the 5th Lord Byron, formerly a captain in the Royal Navy, reenacted many of his earlier exploits, with a large fort and battery, manned by gardeners and gamekeepers who were press-ganged into being soldiers and sailors for the day; while another seafaring family, the Noels, built Fort Henry at Exton Park (*colorplates 41, 42*), perhaps the most ambitious of such buildings to survive.

Sir Francis Dashwood also kept several boats for mock-battles at West Wycombe (*figure 16*), and in 1754 erected "a battery of guns in the form of a fort . . . in order to make a sham-fight between it and the little fleet." However, on this occasion, the captain of one of the vessels "received damage from the wadding of a gun which occasion'd him to spit blood and so put an end to the battle." The Music Temple on an island in the

lake, designed by Nicholas Revett around 1770, had a more peaceful purpose: the inventory taken after Sir Francis's death calls it a theater, and the sight of masquers and musicians ferrying across to it on a summer's evening *(figure 17)*, must have been as picturesque as Watteau's *L'Embarquement pour l'Ile de Cythère*.

Gate lodges had an obvious purpose not only in announcing the visitor's arrival, but also in providing accommodation for gamekeepers or other estate employees. The Pyramid Gate at Castle Howard was used as a guesthouse for visiting gentry who came to see the house, and Kent's Worcester Lodge at Badminton House *(colorplate 8)* has a splendid dining room over the central arch, which is still used for shooting-party lunches. Only a few lodges were conceived as eye-catchers from the house in this way, among them the Corinthian Arch at Stowe, with a sizable

house concealed in each pier, lit by windows hidden on each side. The more advanced theorists of the "Picturesque" style, such as W. S. Gilpin, maintained that gate lodges "should be proportioned in richness and elegance to the house, and should also correspond with it in style." But many architects were happy to use a different idiom, from Adam's elegant Neoclassical gate screen at Syon to the Hindu-Gothic Gateway of Dromona *(colorplate 37)*.

17 • The Music Temple at West Wycombe, *by Thomas Daniell, 1781. Sir Francis Dashwood, Bt.*

A New Design of a Deercote for the Rt Honble Ld Scarsdale.

18 • *A design for a deercote in the Moorish style at Kedleston, Derbyshire, England, by Samuel Wyatt, 1767. The National Trust, London*

Many other "useful" garden buildings were concerned with animals *(figure 18)*—from the Gothick deer houses at Bishop Auckland and Sudbury, to the pyramidal henhouse at Tong, and the extraordinary Grecian temple for pigs at Fyling Hall in Yorkshire. Menageries for rarer animals were also common, many of them remarkable as precursors of the modern zoo. Lions were kept at Hawkstone and Wimpole; storks, raccoons, two young tigers, and a bear were at Horton *(colorplates 67, 68, 69)*. Chambers's famous aviary at Kew, with cages arranged in an octagon around a central pond, looked back to the arrangement of Louis XIV's menagerie at Versailles, and had many imitators—such as Enville in Staffordshire. The huge menagerie and aviary at Woburn Abbey, designed by Humphry Repton in 1804–1805, included a kangaroo enclosure, and had long classical colonnades *(figure 19)* echoing those of Henry Holland's Chinese Dairy *(colorplates 133, 134)*, bordering the pond where rare ducks and other waterfowl were kept. By contrast, the aviary that Repton designed for the Prince Regent at Brighton was in the Indian style, based on a Hindu temple at Bindrabund illustrated in one of the aquatints by Thomas and William Daniell.

The idea of the *ferme ornée*, where the lady of the house could feed her chickens, churn the butter, and even milk a cow, was a self-conscious return to the simple life that grew increasingly popular toward the end of the eighteenth century. One of its earliest protagonists, Philip Southcote, had a poultry house at Woburn Farm in Surrey, which Dr. Pococke described as "in form of a temple, & extends towards the Thames." The seventy-year-old Sir Harry Fetherstonhaugh of Uppark, who married an eighteen-year-old dairymaid—and the 10th Earl of Exeter, who married a farmer's daughter known as the "Cottage Countess"— both had charming tiled milking parlors constructed for their wives; and, of course, Marie Antoinette's famous *hameau* at Versailles was strongly influenced by English prototypes.

Bound up with the early progress of the Romantic Movement, and Rousseau's theories about the "noble savage," this reawakened feeling for untamed nature made many earlier garden buildings seem artificial and contrived. Thus, in his *Red Book* for Blaise Castle (1795–96), Repton suggests a simple cottage in the main view from the house, rather than a more grandiose temple or pavilion *(figure 20)*. "The smoke from the chimney," he writes, "will spread a thin veil along the glen, and produce that kind of vapoury repose over the opposite wood which painters often attempt to describe," concluding that ". . . the idea to be excited is '*La Simplicité soignée*'." For William Shenstone too, a cottage was "a pleasing object . . . on account of the tranquillity that seems to reign there."

The architect and garden designer Thomas Wright of Durham was one of the first to advocate wholly "natural" buildings that seem literally to have grown out of their surroundings. His *Designs for Arbours*, published in 1755, shows one in which the tree-trunk columns and canopy seem to be alive, and bursting into leaf; while one of his *Designs for Grottos*, which came out three years later, shows a rustic mount with a cavern almost swamped by boulders, trees, and moss—and even an owl perched on top for picturesque effect. Wright's fondness for exaggerated forms of rustication, vermiculation, and "frostwork," imitating the primeval forms of weather-beaten stone, also demonstrate an advanced attitude toward buildings as an extension of the natural order.

The hermitage was well-suited to express this concept, and to encourage thoughts of delicious solitude—after the hubbub of the social round, represented by the great house. Perhaps the most famous of these was at Hawkstone in Shropshire, where a resident "friar" was kept to read visitors' palms or to appear rapt in meditation. But in other areas, where real hermits were hard to come by, wax, clockwork, or even stuffed figures were called into service. Horace Walpole disapproved of such frippery (despite some of the more ridiculous aspects of his own rituals at Strawberry Hill), although he made an exception for the one at Hagley: ". . . a hermitage so exactly like those in Sadeler's prints, on the brow of a shady mountain, stealing peeps into the glorious world below."

19 • The Aviary at Woburn Abbey, Bedfordshire, England. From a watercolor in Humphry Repton's Red Book, *1805. By kind permission of the Marquess of Tavistock and the Trustees of the Bedford Estates, Woburn Abbey, England*

20 • *A view of Blaise Castle, Gloucestershire, England. From a watercolor in Humphry Repton's* Red Book, *1795–96. City of Bristol Museum and Art Gallery, England*

Thomas Whateley, in his *Observations on Modern Gardening* (1770), also warned against too much play-acting. "A hermitage," he wrote, "is the habitation of a recluse; it should be distinguished by its solitude and its simplicity; but if it is filled with crucifixes, hourglasses, beads and every other trinket which can be thought of, the attention is diverted from enjoying the retreat to examining the particulars . . . though each be natural, the collection is artificial." However, the practice of keeping "picturesque" characters in garden buildings *(figure 21)* continued at least until the 1850s, when visitors to Alton Towers in Staffordshire were still taken to see the blind harper living in the Swiss Cottage.

Nineteenth-century follies and pleasure pavilions are hardly less numerous than eighteenth-century ones, and although they are generally cruder in execution, and less original in form, there are some notable exceptions: the Egyptian Folly at Biddulph Grange in Staffordshire

(colorplates 13, 14), made almost entirely of topiary; the memorial to Sir Tatton Sykes at Sledmere, like some strange rocket poised for take-off on the Yorkshire Wolds; or the column to the great agriculturalist-Coke of Norfolk at Holkham, with cows' heads where there would normally be volutes. At Alton Towers itself, the amazing assemblage of follies was described by J. C. Loudon as a "labyrinth of terraces, curious architectural walls, trellis-work arbours . . . stone stairs, wooden stairs, turf stairs . . . temples, pagodas, waterfalls, rocks, cottages . . . rock-work, shell-work, root-work, moss houses, old trunks of trees, entire dead trees, etc.," concluding that "no trifling improvement can ever improve what is so far out of the reach of reason."

Even in the twentieth century, the tradition has been upheld by Lord Berners's folly at Faringdon, a tower 140 feet high, with a prospect room at the top, designed by Lord Gerald Wellesley and Trenwith Wills—or by Raymond Erith's circular folly at Gatley in Herefordshire. On the other hand, the greatest achievement of the last twenty-five years has been the restoration of so many earlier temples, eye-catchers, gazebos, and other

eccentric small buildings throughout Britain by the Landmark Trust. Ingeniously adapted for modern life, with bathrooms and kitchens squeezed into a turret here, or a roof-space there, these charming mementos of another age have not only been made safe for future generations, but provide ideal bases for travelers exploring different regions of the country. From the Rococo Gothick of the Gibside Banqueting House *(colorplate 54)* to the Château at Gate Burton, a toy *trianon* in remotest Lincolnshire *(colorplate 53)*—from the Duke of Richmond's hunting box at Charlton in Sussex, to William Jones's sham castle at Clytha in South Wales—there is something for every taste and mood.

Mood, association, magic: these indeed are the essence of follies, so wonderfully conveyed by George Mott's evocative photographs. Covered in ivy, moss, or lichen, built of stone or brick or crumbling stucco, their aspects constantly changing with the weather and the time of day, they have become part of the landscape of England, Ireland, Scotland, and Wales, something we take for granted, that at the same time can suddenly stir the soul. And here I must end on a personal note, remembering the first time I tramped over the fields to my own "eye-catcher," looking blank and shuttered against a gray sky, with the skeletons of great chestnuts behind it on the skyline.

Corrugated iron sheets had replaced the little pyramid roofs of the pavilions, and the lead dome over the central bay window had been stripped off. Inside, the floor was covered with moldy straw, slates had fallen off the roof, and patches of sky showed through gaping holes in the plasterwork ceiling.

At the same time, there was still a feeling of magic in the six Signs of the Zodiac that remained in the cove, recalling the animals of Lord Halifax's eighteenth-century menagerie, in the garlands of flowers and musical instruments, and in the battered figure of Father Time still clinging to the laths, his scythe broken and his wings trimmed. Today, he presides once more over his miniature cosmos (colorplates 67, 68, 69),

surrounded by the four winds, and with urns below, representing the "animals of the four parts of the world"—as Horace Walpole saw them in the 1760s. The garlands around the Signs of the Zodiac show the course of the changing seasons, from the roses and lilies of Cancer and Leo in the bay (the source of light) to the ivy and palms of Capricorn and Aquarius above the fireplace (the source of heat).

It is a room for reflection: a belvedere, with its wide views over trees and grass and water; a banqueting room, for convivial gatherings of old friends; and, at the same time, a hermitage for study and for solitude. No one could ask for more.

ALKERTON GRANGE

Eastington, Gloucestershire, England

The Gazebo

1

The early Georgian brick Gazebo in the garden at Alkerton Grange has an imposing facade with an open segmental pediment and three splendid urns, one borne on the head of a satyr. There is little documentation concerning this garden house, but it may be related to similar structures at Westbury Court and Frampton Court—both of which are located in the same part of the country, and show evidence of Dutch influence.

The interior has fine oak paneling, and it has been carefully restored by the present owners. Over the years, as part of a private residence, the Gazebo has been used variously for rainy-day picnics and afternoon tea, as an oasis for letter writing and reading, and as a convenient "cabana" for those taking advantage of the nearby swimming pool.

1

ALRESFORD

Essex, England

The Quarters

2

The Quarters, a Chinese fishing pavilion, shares its name with the surrounding woods, where Oliver Cromwell's troops were quartered in the seventeenth century, during the English Civil War. It was built by Richard Woods around 1765 for Colonel Rebow, the father-in-law of John Constable's patron. Constable's painting of "the little fishing house" is now in the National Gallery of Victoria, in Melbourne, Australia.

The chinoiserie of the pavilion is restrained and elegant, quite unlike either the authenticity sought by Sir William Chambers, or the Rococo exoticism of William Halfpenny's designs. Formerly perched out over the water, the house contains an octagonal room (that originally served as the dining area), with views over the water on three sides. In the late nineteenth century the building served as a gamekeeper's lodge, but in 1951 it was sensitively restored and converted into a private dwelling for a family long associated with the region.

2

AMESBURY ABBEY

Wiltshire, England

The Chinese House

3 4

3

4

In 1772, Sir William Chambers was commissioned by the Duchess of Queensberry to design the Chinese House at Amesbury Abbey. His work on *Designs of Chinese Buildings* had been published in 1757, and he was a natural choice as the architect to replace the temporary "Chinese" structure in her garden with something more permanent. The pavilion he designed for the Duchess straddles a narrow tributary of the Avon and is "constructed of trapped flint arranged in patterns" with deep projecting eaves and unglazed oval windows.

The Duchess participated in every aspect of the Chinese House's construction and decoration. Her letters indicated her desire to employ a Swiss painter to decorate the interior, but if this was ever carried out no signs of it remain. For years the house was uninhabited and the gardens became overgrown. In *Follies & Grottoes*, Barbara Jones wrote that "there are accounts of an elegant Chinese pavilion and bridge, but these are gone." Fortunately, the pavilion was only hidden in the dense underbrush—it has now been rescued and restored.

Amesbury Abbey is privately owned.

ASKE HALL

North Yorkshire, England

The Temple

5

One of the most ambitious of all Gothick follies, the Temple at Aske Hall was built between 1727 and 1753 for Sir Conyers D'Arcy, probably to designs by Daniel Garrett, a protégé of Lord Burlington and William Kent. The Temple consists of a central octagonal tower joined to smaller side towers—all resting on an arcaded base. Although the frills are decidedly Gothick, the overall structure is Palladian. The main room of the central tower was used for dining, and has naive Gothick plasterwork similar to that in the Gibside Banqueting House (also designed by Garrett).

Aske Hall, a private residence, is the seat of the Marquess of Zetland.

AUDLEY END

Essex, England

The Temple of Victory
6

The Tea-House Bridge
7

A palace in all but name, the great Jacobean mansion at Audley End was one of the largest residences ever built in England, and elicited the wry comment from James I that "it is too much for a King, but it might do very well for a Lord Treasurer." Thomas Howard, Earl of Suffolk and Lord Treasurer to James I, may have lived to regret the grandeur of his establishment, since he eventually found himself imprisoned in the

6

Tower of London, accused of defrauding the King. A substantial portion of the original house was demolished by Sir John Vanbrugh in 1707, but what remains today is impressive by any standards. The magnificent park was laid out by Capability Brown in 1764, and further embellished by Robert Adam.

Designed by Adam in 1771–72, the Temple of Victory was erected to celebrate the conclusion of the Seven Years' War—as well as to close the vista from the house to the west. It bears an inscription that reads:

SACRED TO VICTORY
Eminently Triumphant
In Europe Asia Africa And America
By The Glorious And Unparalleled Success
Of The British Fleets And Armies

In The War Commenced M.DCC.LV
Concluded M.DCC.LXIII
When France And Spain
Making Overtures
To The Crown Of Great Britain
And Yielding
To The Superiority Of Her Arms
PEACE WAS RESTORED

Perhaps Adam's most charming addition to the park at Audley End is the miniature tea-pavilion in the form of a loggia on a classical bridge—a kind of Palladian Bridge *en miniature*

(built in 1782–83), spanning the stream at the north end of the "Elysian Garden." The tea-drinkers, seated around an oval stone table, were afforded a delightful view of the river Cam, the lawn, and a classical bridge in the distance.

The house and park at Audley End are in the care of the Department of the Environment, and are open to the public.

7

BADMINTON HOUSE

Avon, England

Worcester Lodge

8   9   10

Worcester Lodge was built around 1740 by William Kent for the 3rd Duke of Beaufort. In 1754, the peripatetic Bishop Pococke of Ossory recorded a visit to Badminton in his diary: "Worcester Lodge, on the highest ground of the park is a design of Kent. It is a grand room where the duke dines in summer."

Both park guardian and park focus, the Lodge is at once an archetype of the grand gate lodge and an eyecatcher that upstages the main house. It has been described as "a compressed palace rather than . . . a garden house . . ." whose "architectural symbolism is brutally direct: the low pyramidal pavilions house the servants, the high domed room over the arch is for the duke."

9

The interior of the Lodge consists of a lofty dining room reached by a stone staircase enclosed on one side of the gateway arch; the other side houses the service pantry. (Kent's beautiful design for the interior is still preserved at Badminton.) A splendid gilded overmantel mirror with a faceted sunburst is contemporary with the decoration of the room.

Badminton House is the private residence of the Duke of Beaufort.

10

BATH

Avon, England

Lansdown Tower

11

20 Lansdown Crescent,
The Moorish Summerhouse

12

William Beckford (1760–1844) was heir to a colossal fortune and received an enviable education, including music lessons from Wolfgang Amadeus Mozart (then nine years old), and instruction in architecture from Sir William Chambers. As a young man, Beckford wrote a novel, *Vathek*. He also commissioned the construction of an edifice that many consider the definitive folly: Fonthill Abbey. Then, as the result of a scandalous affair with the Honorable William (Kitty) Courtenay—later 9th Earl of Devon—Beckford was ostracized from English society and retired to lead a sybaritic life in Bath.

Perhaps anticipating the restrictions that town life might impose upon him after the spaciousness of Fonthill Abbey, Beckford bought two houses in Lansdown Crescent, as well as a large tract of land behind this fashionable street. H. E. Goodridge, a young architect friend of his, helped to make the houses more comfortable by uniting them via a bridge across the intervening lane.

In 1825–26, Goodridge also designed and built Lansdown Tower at the top of the hill behind the Crescent. The Tower rose to its present height of

11

154 feet through a series of unpremeditated stages, and after much discussion between architect and client. The lantern is an adaptation of the Choragic Monument of Lysicrates in Athens. The Tower contained a drawing room with a collection of objets d'art, a library, and a belvedere that commanded views of

12

the surrounding countryside. The Tower is now part of the cemetery that surrounds it, and is open to the public during the summer. The Moorish Summerhouse is in the private garden behind Beckford's former home—it was probably designed by Beckford himself.

BIDDULPH GRANGE

Staffordshire, England

The Egyptian Folly

13   14

The Egyptian Folly or Court was one of the first of a series of beautiful, bizarre, and witty garden tableaux that formed the nineteenth-century garden at Biddulph Grange. This garden's historical importance is considerable—it is to the last century what Stourhead was to the eighteenth, or Hidcote is to the twentieth.

James Bateman, a distinguished horticulturalist, bought Biddulph Grange in 1842 and created the gardens there during the following twenty-five-year period. His friend, Edward Cooke, R.A., a marine painter, was responsible for many of its unique architectural features. One of these, the Egyptian Folly, constructed partly of stone and partly of clipped yew, has a dark, tomb-like passage leading to an eerily-lit chamber that contains a squat, grimacing "idol." Past this macabre deity, the tunnel emerges from the porch of a Cheshire cottage that forms the other side of the hill, and is the prelude to an entirely new garden experience.

At the eleventh hour, the National Trust has rescued this wonderful garden from certain destruction, and extensive restorations are being planned.

13

14

BLENHEIM PALACE

Oxfordshire, England

The Grand Bridge

15

The Palace and Grand Bridge at Blenheim, built by Sir John Vanbrugh between 1705 and 1716, were designed more in the nature of a public statement than as a private residence. In Vanbrugh's own words, he regarded the Palace "much more as an intended monument to the Queen's glory than as a private habitation of the Duke of Marlborough."

The Grand Bridge marches triumphantly across the valley on the main axis of the Palace, with something of the mounting excitement of a Handel Coronation Ode. The valley was subsequently flooded to provide a series of picturesque lakes, however, robbing the Grand Bridge of the full effect of its powerful design—and coincidentally flooding the magnificent suite of rooms it contained. Vanbrugh and the Duchess came close to blows over his design for the Grand Bridge, and her overbearing philistinism won the day, leading to Vanbrugh's dismissal in 1716. The Duchess commented acidly that the Grand Bridge contained thirty-three rooms, "but that which makes it so much prettier than London Bridge is that you may sit in six rooms and look out the window . . . while the coaches are driving over your head."

Blenheim Palace, the seat of the Duke of Marlborough, is open to the public—the rooms in the Grand Bridge, however, can be reached only via the pleasure boat that plies the lake.

15

BLICKLING HALL
Norfolk, England

The Mausoleum

16

The Egyptian Mausoleum at Blickling was erected in memory of the 2nd Earl of Buckinghamshire, who died in 1793. The design of this grand pyramid in gray stone, based on the Tomb of Gaius Cestius in Rome, was provided by an Italian architect, Joseph Bonomi, who had a successful career in England, and was mentioned by Jane Austen in *Sense and Sensibility*. The door, window, heraldic cow, hound, and bull rest on a base forty-five feet square. The monument was meant to be seen at the end of a wide avenue of yews.

Blickling Hall is owned by the National Trust, and is open to the public.

BODNANT
Gwynedd, Wales

The Pin Mill

17

The garden at Bodnant is one of the glories of Wales. It was begun in 1875, although the major work was carried out early in this century by the 2nd Lord Aberconway, who laid out a series of Italianate terraces. In 1938, he bought the Pin Mill to adorn the Canal Terrace. Originally a garden house at Woodchester, Gloucestershire, England, the Pin Mill was built in 1730 and attached to an Elizabethan residence. Before making the journey to Bodnant, this delightful building served as a mill for the manufacture of pins, and also as a tannery. The elegant room in the tower above the loggia has been used for picnics, as well as for tea and cocktail parties.

Bodnant belongs to the National Trust, and is open to the public.

16

BOUGHTON HOUSE

Northamptonshire, England

The Chinese Tent
18

The Chinese Tent preserved at Boughton House is a unique example of a collapsible garden pavilion made of oilskin, that was produced in London in the mid-eighteenth century. The tent has a wooden frame, and panels that open or close to provide protection from the sun and wind. The tent was used in the garden of the London house of the Montagu Douglas Scott family, and can be seen there in Canaletto's *View of the Thames from Richmond House,* now at Goodwood.

Boughton House, one of the residences of the Duke of Buccleuch and Queensberry, is open to the public.

BOWOOD

Wiltshire, England

The Mausoleum
19

The Doric Temple
20

19

20

The Mausoleum was designed by Robert Adam in 1761, as a monument to the 1st Earl of Shelburne. The somber character of the design, in keeping with its function, is unlike Adam's lighter domestic vein, but the building has a thoughtful sculptural quality unique in his work. The particularly fine interior has a screen of columns supporting an entablature that runs around the four walls, framing the arched recesses intended for the family tombs.

The Doric Temple serves both as a garden seat from which to view the house across the lake, and as a focal point in the landscape composition of Capability Brown.

Bowood is the residence of the Lansdowne family, and is open to the public.

BRAMHAM PARK

West Yorkshire, England

The Gothic Temple

21   22

Paine's Temple

23

The garden at Bramham Park, begun in 1699 by Robert Benson (later Lord Bingley), is regarded as the outstanding English example of the French garden style of Le Nôtre. High beech hedges form *allées* with *salles de verdure* and geometric reflecting pools interspersed with garden buildings that were added later, between 1750 and 1770.

The Gothic Temple or Octagon was built in 1750, in accordance with a design from Batty Langley's *Gothic Architecture improved by Rules and Proportions in many Grand Designs* of 1742. The Temple stands on a stretch of greensward known as the Bowling Green, and served both as a summerhouse and as a water tower for

domestic use. The interior is embellished with Gothick plasterwork, and is furnished with stools and tables decorated with heraldic motifs.

21

22

The vista along the Broad Walk is closed by James Paine's Temple (c. 1760), a delightfully-proportioned structure composed of a balustraded Ionic portico fronting a rectangular *cella* with five-sided wings. The building seems to have been used for diverse activities over the years. Originally conceived as an orangery or banqueting house, it was consecrated as a chapel in the early part of this century.

Bramham Park has belonged to the same family for nine generations, and is open to the public.

BROCKLESBY PARK

Lincolnshire, England

The Mausoleum

24

The 1st Earl of Yarborough commissioned James Wyatt to design a Mausoleum for his young wife, who had died at the age of thirty-three. Widely considered Wyatt's masterpiece, this stunning building was erected between 1787 and 1792. The design of the Mausoleum is based on the Temple of Vesta at Tivoli, by way of Bramante's *Tempietto* in Rome.

Standing on a hill, the Mausoleum is a splendid eye-catcher in the park laid out by Capability Brown in 1771.

The Mausoleum belongs to the Earl of Yarborough, and is open by appointment.

BURGHLEY HOUSE

Cambridgeshire, England

The Bath House

25

Capability Brown made extensive changes in the landscape surrounding Burghley, at the behest of the 9th Earl of Exeter—it was Brown's last great work. He designed a number of structures for the park, among them are the Lion Bridge, a Gothick greenhouse, an icehouse, a dairy, and a Jacobean Bath House.

The Bath House, really a summerhouse, occupies a charming position on the lake, amid a small grove of cedars. It was built in 1756, and represents one of the earliest examples of Jacobean Revival in the country. Throughout the years it has been used for different activities: as a writing room, a morning room in which to receive visitors, and more recently, as a museum for family collections.

Burghley House, owned by a private family trust, is open to the public.

24

CASTLE HOWARD

North Yorkshire, England

The Temple of the Four Winds
26

The Mausoleum
27

Castle Howard offers some of "the grandest scenes of rural magnificence," according to Horace Walpole, who also wrote that "at one view" it was possible to see "a palace, a town, a fortified city, temples on high places, woods worthy of being each a metropolis of the Druids, the noblest lawn in the world fenced by half the horizon, and a mausoleum that would tempt one to be buried alive."

26

27

The Temple of the Four Winds was designed by Sir John Vanbrugh in 1724–26, with four Ionic porticoes and a dome with a square lantern. The roofline is enlivened by urns and finials. The interior has scagliola decoration, busts of Roman notables, and an inlaid marble floor.

The Mausoleum, designed by Nicholas Hawksmoor in 1728–29, is one of the glories of the English Baroque, an impassioned, romantic valedictory to a classical Rome the architect never visited. Although it was subjected to many alterations, and remained unfinished at Hawksmoor's death in 1736, it is comparable in importance to some of Wren's greatest buildings.

Castle Howard is open to the public, following a long tradition noted in a survey of 1829, which describes "the noble proprietor . . . admitting the public to view this elegant repository."

CHATELHERAULT

Renfrewshire, Scotland

The Dog Kennel

28

The long screen of buildings (280 feet) that originally closed a view from the now-vanished palace of the Dukes of Hamilton, derives its name from Chatelherault in France because, while it was under construction, the family was engaged in reclaiming a French dukedom of that name, which was thought to have been conferred on an ancestor of theirs in 1549. The structure is described, perhaps facetiously, as a "Dogg Kennell" on the elevation that appeared in *Vitruvius Scoticus*. Built around 1732 to the designs of William Adam, the father of Robert Adam, it has served the multiple functions of kennel, summerhouse, banqueting house, hunting lodge, menagerie, and eye-catcher.

The Scottish Government acquired this magnificent folly in 1978, and has spent ten years overseeing its painstaking restoration. The rooms provided for the Duke and Duchess, which had been richly decorated in stucco by Thomas Clayton, have all been restored, in some cases from photographs taken in 1919. The building and grounds are open to the public.

CLAREMONT

Esher, Surrey, England

The Belvedere
29

The landscape garden of Claremont House is one of the earliest of its kind to have survived, and it contains such features as an earthwork amphitheater designed by Charles Bridgeman, an island pavilion by William Kent, and a grotto.

The Belvedere, designed by Sir John Vanbrugh, commanded views of the entire garden and the surrounding countryside. In 1716 it was equipped with a table for playing hazard (a dice game), and a pantry, from which the butler served refreshment. The Belvedere was originally painted white.

After many vicissitudes, the garden at Claremont was acquired by the National Trust, and brilliantly restored. It is open to the public.

30

COLEBY HALL

Lincolnshire, England

Temple of Romulus and Remus
30

Sir William Chambers designed the Temple of Romulus and Remus sometime around 1762 for his friend and traveling companion, Thomas Scrope, with whom he had "viewed old Rome." Occupying a grassy knoll at the end of a drive, the circular Temple has two pedimented porches with Tuscan columns and a pair of projecting apses. The interior of the dome has a design of coffers diminishing in size toward the center — a device used in the Pantheon in Rome.

Coleby Hall is a private residence; the Temple may be seen by prior permission.

CORSHAM COURT

Wiltshire, England

The Bath House

31   32

The Gothick Bath House at Corsham Court was designed by Capability Brown in 1760 as part of a major transformation of the house and grounds; it consists of a room lit by stained-glass windows, over an open loggia. Therapeutic cold baths were in vogue throughout the eighteenth century, largely as a result of Dr. Oliver's treatise, *A Practical Dissertation on the Bath Waters* (1707). Such baths were meant to be taken only infrequently, and thus would become the focal point of a particular outing to a grotto or pavilion in the park of a country house.

The garden at Corsham Court also contains a highly eccentric nineteenth-century folly wall built to resemble a ruined medieval castle; it stands adjacent to the Bath House at the bottom of the walled garden.

Corsham Court is the home of Lord Methuen, and is open to the public.

32

CROOME COURT

Worcestershire, England

The Rotunda

33   34   35

In 1750, the 6th Earl of Coventry commissioned Capability Brown to redesign his house and landscape his large estate at Croome Court—an imposing, if somewhat charmless, Palladian hulk of a building and a thoroughly delightful park were the result. Robert Adam also worked at Croome Court over a twenty-year period from 1760 onward, as indicated by his carefully-rendered accounts to Lord Coventry. Adam designed much of the interior of the house and several pleasure buildings for the park.

33

The Rotunda is not one of the buildings mentioned in Adam's accounts, and this lovely round temple may be a composite of Brown's and Adam's designs. The robust plaster heads and swags of the interior suggest an earlier stylistic milieu than the chaste plaques on the exterior.

Heavy death duties forced the breakup of the Coventry Estate, and Croome Court was purchased by the International Society of Krishna Consciousness, whose members used the Rotunda for meditation. Recently, the property changed hands again, and is said to be destined for meticulous restoration and conversion into living quarters.

34

DOWNHILL

County Derry, Northern Ireland

The Mussenden Temple

36

Frederick Augustus Hervey, 4th Earl of Bristol, Bishop of Derry (1730–1803), was addicted to women and building—particularly to building in the round. Two of his palatial residences, Ickworth in Suffolk, England, and Ballyscullion in County Derry, Northern Ireland (now demolished), were designed with circular, or elliptical, domed main buildings. Rich and eccentric, the Earl-Bishop may have been inspired in his rotundifications by images of classical buildings such as the Pantheon in Rome, or by an early encounter with Belle Isle on Lake Windermere in England.

After traveling extensively in Italy (and so extravagantly that Bristol Hotels all over Europe bear his name), he asked John Soane to provide drawings of the Temple of Vesta at Tivoli, and he is said to have attempted to purchase the ruined temple itself from an innkeeper on whose property it stood. Thus, in 1785, a circular temple similar in design to the one at Tivoli was completed on the Bishop's coastal estate at Downhill; it is likely that Michael Shanahan of Cork, who had traveled with the Bishop on the continent during the early 1770s (and was the architect responsible for the Bishop's great house on the same property), was the designer. The Mussenden Temple was intended to commemorate the Bishop's attractive young kinswoman, Frideswide Bruce, the widow of Daniel Mussenden of Larchfield in County Down, Northern Ireland.

Perched precariously on a rocky precipice overlooking the Atlantic, the site of the Mussenden Temple must be one of the most dramatic anywhere. Built of cut stone, it measures forty feet in diameter, and consists of a single domed room surrounded by sixteen attached Corinthian columns separated by carved swags. The entablature contains a Latin inscription from Lucretius's *De Rerum Natura:* *"Suave, mari magno turbantibus aequora ventis, e terra magnum alterius spectare laborem."* ("Sweet it is, when on the high seas the winds are lashing the waters, to gaze from the land on another's struggles.") The arms of the Hervey family and of the See of Derry are inscribed in an escutcheon over the door. The leaded dome is capped by a finial in the form of a stone urn. The interior, originally a library but now quite bare, still retains traces of its blue and gilt decoration, and once had a coffered ceiling. A visitor to Downhill in 1801 described the setting: "The Bishop has built a handsome Grecian temple full of valuable but mouldering books, some on shelves and some piled in disorder upon the floor. Since no provision was made for heating, it can have been used only in the summer months . . . on occasions, the wind on the plateau was so strong that servants could get back to the house only on hands and knees." In the vaulted brick crypt below, the tolerant Earl-Bishop allowed Catholics to celebrate Mass, specifying in his will that the practice should continue after his death.

The isolated situation of the Mussenden Temple, with three windows looking out to sea and the background roar of the surf always present, makes it an ideal spot for study or contemplation, although the Earl-Bishop apparently had little time for either pursuit, since he was almost constantly on the move among his various properties or touring Italy in search of decorative acquisitions for his mansions.

The Mussenden Temple is the best preserved of the buildings at Downhill, since the main house is now an empty shell. There also remain a mausoleum copied after the Roman Temple of the Julii at St. Rémy, in Provence, and the ruins of Lady Erne's Seat (the Bishop's eldest daughter Mary married the 1st Lord Erne), a circular building with windows on three sides, also on a promontory jutting into the Atlantic.

DROMONA

County Waterford, Ireland

The Hindu-Gothic Gateway
37

The Hindu-Gothic Gateway at Dromona was built as a temporary structure (perhaps in wood or papier-mâché), to celebrate the marriage of Henry Villiers-Stuart and Theresia Pauline Ott of Vienna in 1826. It is said that the young couple were so delighted with it that they had the Gateway reconstructed in durable materials to be used as a gate-lodge.

The Oriental fantasies of the Brighton Pavilion had exercised considerable influence in England, but the Hindu-Gothic Gateway at Dromona would seem to have been its only descendant in Ireland. It would no longer even exist if it had not been for a rescue operation carried out by the Irish Georgian Society in 1968. However, it has since fallen prey to vandalism (ever a problem with secluded monuments), and is in danger of extinction once again.

37

DUNMORE PARK

Stirlingshire, Scotland

The Pineapple

38   39   40

The Pineapple was built in 1761
for Lord Dunmore by an unknown
architect. Pineapples had been
cultivated in Scotland since the early
eighteenth century, and the choice of
one for the design of a garden house
may have been influenced by nothing
more recherché than the fruit's aes-
thetically satisfying appearance. If
symbolism must be sought, perhaps
one could hypothesize a representa-
tion of man's triumph over the
elements—an exotic tropical fruit
flourishing in the chilly North.

38

Dunmore Park · continued

The Pineapple, fifty feet high, is actually the top half of a banqueting house that stands on the wall dividing two levels: an orchard on the lower side, a walled garden on the upper.

From top to bottom, the design and execution of the Pineapple is faultlessly, ingeniously elegant. The base has ogee-arched windows that flow harmoniously into a cushion of exuberantly-carved leaves which, in turn, support rows of segments that diminish in size up to a crown of crisp, arched, serrated leaves. The

segments and leaves are individually drained to prevent any disastrous buildup of ice during the winter.

At orchard level there is an open, pedimented porch. In contrast to the exterior, the single room inside the

Pineapple is quite simple. The Pineapple, and its surrounding grounds, were given to the National Trust for Scotland, and they are open to the public. (The Landmark Trust has leased and restored the building, and it is available for short-term holiday rentals.)

39

40

EXTON PARK

Leicestershire, England

Fort Henry

41   42

The fishing pavilion on an ornamental lake in Exton Park was built by, and named after, Henry, 6th Earl of Gainsborough, who is reputed to have reenacted the great sea battles of his day on the lake, using miniature men-of-war crewed by his servants and tenants.

The actual construction of this pinnacled Gothick pleasure-house is difficult to pinpoint, since the family papers were destroyed in a fire in 1810, but on stylistic grounds it was probably built in the 1790s or early 1800s. The Fort has a fine interior consisting of a large central room with two smaller rooms on either side. There is a boathouse underneath, at water level.

On the hill behind Fort Henry is the ruin of an extremely rare garden house made entirely of tree bark. The present Lord Gainsborough, having restored Fort Henry to its original splendor, is undertaking the difficult rescue operation on the Bark Temple, as well.

Fort Henry is open to the public by special prior arrangement.

41

42

FARNBOROUGH HALL

Warwickshire, England

The Oval Pavilion

43 44

Farnborough Hall was built soon after the Holbech family took possession of the property in 1684. The Terrace Walk of 1751, with spectacular views over the surrounding countryside, rises gently from the south front of the house, along the ridge, past two classical temples, and culminates after three-quarters of a mile at an obelisk. It has often been compared with the Terrace at Rievaulx in Yorkshire as two of the most ambitious landscaping projects of their kind. Both are tributes to the

43

"Picturesque" movement, with which William Holbech and his neighbor, Sanderson Miller, the gentleman architect, were closely allied. The Ionic Temple and the Oval Pavilion (sometimes called the Prospect Tower) have generally been attributed to Miller, who was also advising Lord Lyttelton at Hagley during that same period.

The Oval Pavilion is formed of an open loggia with four Tuscan columns around a stone table, with a stone staircase at the rear that leads up to a room of extraordinary beauty. Its domed ceiling and curved walls are decorated with plaster rocaille, probably by the Yorkshire master of stucco, William Perritt, who executed the similar decoration in the house.

The National Trust acquired Farnborough and 344 surrounding acres in 1960 (although the Holbech family continues to occupy the house). The Terrace Walk and the house are open to the public.

44

FAWLEY COURT

Buckinghamshire, England

The Island Temple

45

The fishing lodge on Temple Island in the Thames at Remenham, Berkshire, was built by James Wyatt around 1771 as an eye-catcher—Fawley Court being on the other side of the river (and, incidentally, in the contiguous county of Buckinghamshire).

Originally, the Temple contained one large room "ornamented in a very expensive manner" in the "Etruscan style." These wall decorations may have been designed by Wyatt himself, and are thought to be among the earliest examples of this kind of decoration in the country. A circular tempietto surmounts the single room, behind which there are later additions. The Temple is familiar to boating enthusiasts since it marks the mile-long course from Henley, and is a highly-favored vantage point for watching the races.

Together with the island upon which it stands, the Temple is now the property of the Henley Royal Regatta.

FONTHILL GIFFORD

Wiltshire, England

The Triumphal Arch

46 47

The Triumphal Arch at Fonthill Gifford (whose design has been attributed, erroneously, to Inigo Jones), seems to have been the work of a London master builder named Hoare. It was constructed between 1757 and 1770 as the gateway to William Beckford's childhood home, Fonthill Splendens, to which it formed an imperious prelude. Splendens was pulled down by Beckford in 1807 after he had moved into Fonthill Abbey, the definitive English folly designed by James Wyatt (which collapsed under its own weight in 1825).

The tripartite composition of the Fonthill gateway has heavy bands of vermiculated rustication forming a huge human face in the keystone of the arch. The Triumphal Arch, successively the gateway to two palaces, straddles a public road and is now a small and charming private house.

46

47

FRAMPTON COURT

Gloucestershire, England

The Gothick Orangery

48 49 50 51

The designer of the mid-eighteenth-century Gothick Orangery at Frampton Court is not known, but there is a resemblance in form to designs featured in William and John Halfpenny's *Chinese and Gothic Architecture Properly Ornamented* (1752). The Orangery closes the view along an ornamental canal and is composed of two octagons joined by a rectangular hall, behind which is an octagonal tower containing a staircase.

The detail of the Orangery is exceptional: the interior is carefully planned and finely executed with ogee-arched door frames, a terracotta fireplace with contemporary Dutch tiles, and a superb cantilevered stone staircase.

Frampton Court and its gardens are open to the public by special arrangement with the owner.

49

50

51

GARRICK'S VILLA

Middlesex, England

The Shakespeare Temple
52

The actor, playwright, and producer of Shakespeare's plays, David Garrick (1717–79), was the subject of many contemporary tributes and descriptions. His house at Hampton Court was a meeting place for the artistic and literary figures of his time. In 1756, he commissioned a statue of Shakespeare from the sculptor, Roubiliac, and the riverside summerhouse was devised especially to house it.

Horace Walpole wrote in 1756: "John and I are just going to Garrick's with a grove of cypresses in our hands, like the Kentish men at the conquest.

He has built a Temple to his master Shakespeare, and I am going to adorn the outside, since his modesty would not let me decorate it within, as I proposed, with these mottoes:

Quod spiro et placeo, si placeo, tuum est.
—*Horace, Carm. IV iii, 24.*

(That I am inspired and that my productions please, if they do, is due to you.)

"That I Spirit have and nature,
That sense breathes in ev'ry feature,
That I please, if please I do,
Shakespeare, all I owe to you.
Adieu!"

The octagonal shell and Ionic portico were finished, and the lead dome ready to be put in place, when Garrick asked Capability Brown's advice about how to deal with the public road between his house and the Thames-side Temple. Brown suggested a tunnel, which was promptly seconded by Dr. Johnson: "David, David, what can't be overdone, may be underdone."

The riverside plot, with the Shakespeare Temple, is now a public park.

GATE BURTON

Lincolnshire, England

The Château

53

The so-called Château perched on a pleasantly-wooded site above the river Trent in the park of Gate Burton Hall constitutes one of those delightful architectural enigmas that dot the English countryside, often seen fleetingly from a car or train window, and which so often prove to have been the work of an inspired provincial architect or builder.

The Château was built in 1747 by a young architect, John Platt, for Thomas Hutton, a wealthy lawyer from Gainsborough. Hutton had recently bought the entire estate of Gate Burton from the Earl of Abingdon, whose affairs he managed. As there was no suitable house on the property, he built the Château as a temporary country cottage. In the words of one of his sons, "he used to retire from the Business of his office at Gainsborough, from a Saturday Evening until the Monday Morning." He would probably have had his rooms on the first floor, with a kitchen and servant's room below.

After 1768, when Gate Burton Hall was completed, the Château came to be used as a summerhouse for family *fêtes champêtres*, and as a shooting box. Recently acquired by the Landmark Trust, it has been meticulously restored, and is rented for brief periods as a country retreat.

53

GIBSIDE

Tyne and Wear, England

The Banqueting House

54

The Gothick Banqueting House on the Gibside estate was built in 1751 by Daniel Garrett. The building is remarkably elaborate, consisting of a "Great Room" thirty-two feet long with matching apses, one formed by the bow on the front. There is a kitchen and an anteroom on either side of the recessed portico at the back of the building.

Ironically, the coal mining that financed the building at Gibside also led to the collapse of the main house and the abandonment of the estate, as a result of subsidence in the subterranean mines. The Banqueting House had fallen into abject disrepair—the lovely Gothick plasterwork of the interior almost entirely lost—when it was acquired by that champion of garden buildings, the Landmark Trust. It has since been restored, and made available for holiday rentals.

GLEVERING HALL

Suffolk, England

The Orangery

55   56   57   58

The desire to cultivate oranges, even under difficult conditions, was the generative force behind the venerable English tradition of growing plants under glass, and "orangery" has persisted as a name for any elaborate, freestanding greenhouse or conservatory.

56

55

57

The Orangery at Glevering Hall was built in the 1830s by Decimus Burton, who had designed many distinguished buildings in London and Manchester. In fact, the Orangery has a rather urban look—its outline having been inspired by such Greek Revival essays as Wilkins's Downing College in Cambridge.

The Orangery has a fine, nineteenth-century cast-iron interior, with a glass dome supported by palm-tree columns.

Glevering Hall is a private residence; the Orangery may be viewed by prior arrangement.

GOODWOOD HOUSE

West Sussex, England

Carné's Seat

59   60

Tradition has it that Carné's Seat is named for a certain M. de Carné, an aged French servant of Louise de Kerouaille, who is said to have lived in a cottage on the site. This elegant banqueting house was built around 1743 for the 2nd Duke of Richmond by Roger Morris. George Vertue, who visited Goodwood in 1747, described it as "a beautiful building of stone, fronted with an Archade, rooms and other agreeable conveniences for to entertain company. & over it a most beautifull dineing room—finely adorned with stucco's carvings marbles &c in the finest and most elegant taste. here I had the pleasure to accompany thire graces—with other Gentlemen to drink tea &c their coaches and equipages attending in great magnificence and state."

The present Duke of Richmond uses Carné's Seat as a painter's studio.

HALL BARN

Buckinghamshire, England

The Temple of Venus

61

The garden of Hall Barn was originally laid out by the poet Edmund Waller after 1651, and later enlarged (as well as embellished) by the poet's grandson and the latter's stepfather, John Aislabie, Chancellor of the Exchequer (see Studley Royal).

The Temple of Venus was designed by Colen Campbell during the period that he worked on Hall Barn House in the 1720s. The Temple is an open rotunda that forms the centerpiece for a system of radial walks. Inside the dome are dancing cherubs with garlands, possibly by the Italian workers in stucco, Artari and Bagutti.

Hall Barn is the private residence of Lord Burnham.

61

HARRISTOWN HOUSE

County Kildare, Ireland

The Chinese House

62 63

62

The Chinese House was built sometime before 1738 for the garden at Stowe, Buckinghamshire; it is one of the earliest Chinese pavilions in Ireland or Great Britain. Seeley's engraving of 1750 shows the House at Stowe, standing on stilts in an ornamental pond. In 1751, Bishop Pococke noted that "the Chinese House is taken away," and it seems that the pavilion was moved to the garden of Wotton House, also in Buckinghamshire, where it remained until the 1950s when it became, briefly, a boys' school. Finally, the previous owners of Wotton transported the Chinese House across the Irish Sea, and up the Liffey, to its present site in County Kildare.

The House is decorated with paintings of Chinese scenes by Francesco Sleter, which have been repainted over the years, most recently by Percy Willats.

Harristown House is a private residence.

63

HOLKHAM HALL
Norfolk, England

The Temple
64

The Triumphal Arch
65

The Temple in the Obelisk Wood at Holkham was designed by William Kent for Thomas Coke (later 1st Earl of Leicester), and erected in 1730–35. It consists of a domed octagon with an Ionic portico and side wings. The interior was meant to house plaster replicas of classical sculpture in niches. The Temple is now used for summer picnics and other festive gatherings.

William Kent also designed the Triumphal Arch in the park at Holkham, through which suitably awed visitors made their way up the impressive drive to Coke's magnificent house. The original design for the Arch shows a large, tripartite structure with rusticated pyramids over the side openings, rather like Worcester Lodge. The Triumphal Arch was erected by Matthew Bret-

tingham with modifications that included the elimination of the pyramids.

The Triumphal Arch has been made into a comfortable country retreat by the architect Nicholas Hills.

Holkham Hall is the seat of the Earls of Leicester, and is open to the public.

64

HORTON

Dorset, England

Horton Tower

66

A true folly, Horton Tower does not appear to have been built for any clear purpose. It has been attributed to the architect Thomas Archer, perhaps because it bears a remote resemblance to the garden pavilion he built at Wrest Park. There is evidence, however, that this imposing eye-catcher, standing 140 feet high, was built around 1765 by a local squire, Humphrey Sturt, who may have used it as an observatory and/or a vantage point from which to watch deer on Cranborne Chase.

Horton Tower is accessible to the public.

66

HORTON

Northamptonshire, England

The Menagerie

67 68 69

The Menagerie was built in the 1750s by Thomas Wright for Lord Halifax. It was conceived as an omnibus garden structure to serve as zoo, eye-catcher, and banqueting house.

Thomas Wright's long composition sets a villa-like central building, with lower wings, between pavilions that are connected by screen-walls to conceal the area where Lord Halifax kept a private zoo, described by Horace Walpole in 1763 as containing "many basons of gold fish . . . several curious birds and beasts . . . Raccoons that breed there much . . . two hogs from the Havannah with navels on their backs . . . two uncommon Martins . . . a kind of Ermine . . . doves from Guadaloupe with blue heads and a milk white streak crossing their cheeks." Four of the six original "basons" survive in the garden behind the Menagerie.

67

Horton Northants • continued

The central block of the Menagerie contains splendid plasterwork attributed to Thomas Roberts of Oxford, including the Signs of the Zodiac, Father Time, and a sunburst with the mask of Apollo. From this richly-decorated room with its broad, deep, three-windowed bay, Lord Halifax must have been able to admire many a postprandial sunset over his splendid mansion across the park.

The Menagerie had become derelict when Gervase Jackson-Stops rescued and restored it with the help of the artist and designer, Christopher Hobbs, who renewed much of the plasterwork.

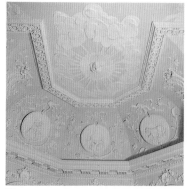

69

HOUGHTON HALL

Norfolk, England

The Water House

70

Although Sir Robert Walpole had been a successful statesman, he remained a countryman at heart, retiring happily to his magnificent estate at Houghton after he had completed his last term as Prime Minister (1721–42). Walpole plowed back the fortune he had made in politics into a princely house and park that remain much as he left them at his death in 1745.

The Water House, on a hill at some distance from the main house, is a building wherein water was raised and stored in tanks for use on the estate. The designs for this "Palladian jewel," (which are in the Metropolitan Museum of Art, New York) are ascribed to the Earl of Pembroke in a note by Walpole's son Horace: "The Water-House in the Park; design'd by Henry Lord Herbert, afterwards Earl of Pembroke,"

suggesting that the building was designed before Lord Herbert became Earl of Pembroke in 1733. The ingenious arrangement of two back-to-back loggias over a rusticated base provided a place for the water-tanks below, and two elegant vantage points above.

Houghton Hall, the seat of the Marquess of Cholmondeley, is open to the public.

KEDLESTON HALL

Derbyshire, England

The Fishing Room

71   72   73   74

The house and park at Kedleston display two sides of Robert Adam's genius: the house, built in the 1760s when he was fresh from his Italian travels, shows the architect at his most inventive, while the sketches of the park made in 1759–60 afford a rare glimpse of Adam as landscape gardener. The park has several small buildings designed by him, including the North Lodge, in the form of a triumphal arch, and a balustraded bridge and cascade. But the Fishing Room-cum-boathouse-cum-cold-bath at the edge of the upper lake is a gem among eighteenth-century garden buildings.

Built in 1771, the Fishing Room is a tripartite structure consisting of a double-storied, pedimented central section with a Venetian window, and flanked by lower wings for mooring boats. The entrance to the Fishing Room is set in an apsidal recess. Inside, there is a curving flight of stone steps to the right and the left, which descend to the chamber beneath the main room of the house, within which an underground spring emerges from the hillside into a stone basin let into the floor, and from there into the lake. The mellifluous gurgle in the vaulted chamber is memorable.

71

72

The main chamber of the Fishing Room, used for both fishing and dining, is decorated with four oil paintings of fish, a marble statue of Diana, an elegant chimneypiece, as well as plaques and bands of classical motifs in shallow relief. A row of clasps for fishing rods is fixed to one wall.

Kedleston Hall is owned by the National Trust and is open to the public, although it also remains the home of the present Viscount Scarsdale and his family.

73

MARGAM

West Glamorgan, Wales

The Orangery

75 76

When Philip II of Spain sent a gift of orange trees to Queen Elizabeth I, the ship was wrecked off the coast of West Glamorgan. Tradition has it that the salvaged trees were housed at Margam in the predecessor of what was destined to be the largest building of its kind in the British Isles.

After Thomas Mansel Talbot demolished the dilapidated family mansion in 1787, he used much of its timber and stonework to build the impressive Georgian Orangery, which is almost 300 feet in length. The design, by Anthony Keck, consists of a long, low building with twenty-eight heavily rusticated bays. To alleviate the monotony produced by such a repetitive design, the four central bays were made to protrude slightly, and then surmounted by a section of ornamented parapet. There are square, pedimented pavilions at either end, and the roofline is enlivened with stone urns.

Margam Park and the Orangery are in the care of the West Glamorgan County Council, and both are open to the public.

75

76

MARINO

Dublin, Ireland

The Casino

77 78 79

A landmark in Neoclassical architecture, the Casino at Marino was designed by Sir William Chambers in 1759 for the 1st Earl of Charlemont. The Casino, regarded by many as the finest garden building of its kind in Europe, was a very expensive undertaking—such was the solicitude lavished upon its construction that Lord Charlemont was forced to sell land elsewhere in the country to pay for its completion.

The plan of the Casino, a Greek cross, is ingeniously deployed to provide both private and public areas one might usually expect only in a much larger building. The scale is deceptive—even from a slight distance the Casino appears toylike, as if its delightful urn-chimneys were about to emit the perfumed smoke of a pastille burner.

Marino Casino • continued

Sir William Chambers in his *Treatise* of 1791 published an elevation and plan of the Casino, and remarked that it "was built by Mr. Verpyle with great neatness and taste, after models made here and instructions sent from hence." The rooms in the basement are designated as kitchen, scullery, pantry, butler's pantry, wine cellar, servants' hall, and ale cellar. On the *piano nobile* there is an apsed vestibule leading to the saloon, a small study, a bedroom, and the narrow staircase. The top floor (not illustrated by Chambers) contains a grand state bedroom, a second bedroom, a dressing room, a valet's room, and stairs leading to a gazebo on the roof. The marquetry floors of the principal rooms have geometric patterns inlaid in exotic woods.

The exterior of the Casino is decorated with bas-reliefs by Cipriani and sculpted lions by Joseph Wilton, based on those in the Villa Borghese in Rome.

The Casino, a National Monument, is administered by the Office of Public Works, and—having been under restoration since 1972—is now open to the public.

78

79

MELFORD HALL

Suffolk, England

The Pavilion

80

The Melford Hall property includes a rare and fine example of a mid-sixteenth-century garden house. The octagonal Tudor pavilion forms the northwest corner of a mellow brick garden wall. Each of the eight faces has a pointed gable crowned by a slender turret; it may originally have been a guardhouse from which it was possible to observe the two moats and the main road.

The upper octagonal room has eighteenth-century paneling that was originally painted dark green and had gilded moldings. The presence of a furnace on the ground floor probably means that the pavilion was used as an orangery in the eighteenth century. The ground floor is entered directly from the garden at the bottom of the wall, while the upper room has a flight of stone steps leading to a hooded porch with fluted columns.

Melford Hall, in the village of Long Melford, is a property of the National Trust, and is open to the public.

80

MILTON PARK

Northamptonshire, England

The Gothick Lodge

81

The Kennels

82

The Gothick Lodge in the park at Milton, the seat of the Earls Fitzwilliam, has sometimes been attributed to Sir William Chambers, but it seems more likely that Humphry Repton, who remodeled the garden in 1791, designed it—possibly in association with John Nash. The Lodge has a polygonal front with a rose window, and a gable with a Norman scallop frieze inspired by a similar frieze on Peterborough Cathedral. The chimneys exit via an octagonal turret at the back of the house.

The Kennels, a buttressed and embattled sham "ruin," has been attributed to Chambers. It was built in 1767, and still houses one of the most venerable packs of dogs in the country, hounds having been kenneled at Milton since medieval times.

Milton Park is the private residence of the Countess Fitzwilliam.

82

81

MONTACUTE HOUSE

Somerset, England

The Pavilions

83

Montacute House was built in the last decade of the sixteenth century for Sir Edward Phelips, a distinguished lawyer and parliamentarian. It is one of the best preserved and most exquisite Elizabethan mansions extant. The lovely garden Pavilions are located at the corners of what was the forecourt entrance to the house; a large and impressive gatehouse originally stood between them, but it has long since disappeared. The Pavilions have two stories, and the upper chambers were reportedly furnished as bedrooms (according to an account dated 1638). The Pavilions have ogee roofs, turrets, and obelisks—all elements used elsewhere in the decoration of the house. Buildings of this type are sometimes to be found on the flat roofs of the great Elizabethan mansions, and were often used as banqueting rooms where dessert could be served while the main dining-hall was being cleared for after-dinner entertainments and diversions.

Montacute House is a property of the National Trust, and is open to the public.

83

MOUNT STEWART

County Down, Northern Ireland

The Temple of the Winds

84 85

A nodding acquaintance with the Classical world was an obligatory attribute of the eighteenth-century gentleman, and the manifestation of this familiarity might be a piece of antiquity in one's own backyard — temples, ruined aqueducts, and miniature pantheons all found their way into the gardens of those who could afford them. One of the source books for ancient buildings was James Stuart and Nicholas Revett's *Antiquities of Athens* (the first volume of which was published in 1762). James "Athenian" Stuart may be credited with the introduction of "Greek Revival" in the British Isles as a result of his faithful copies of complete Greek structures such as the Doric Temple at Hagley Park, built in 1758. Stuart also designed archaeologically correct versions of other famous antique monuments: the Arch of Hadrian in Athens, the Monument of Lysicrates, and the Tower of Andronicus Cyrrhestes (better known as the Tower of the Winds); all were published in his *Antiquities*.

No Tower of the Winds to be found in any other British garden is quite as correct a version as the one at Mount Stewart in Northern Ireland, built in 1782 for the future 1st Marquess of Londonderry by James "Athenian" Stuart. The octagonal, two-storied banqueting house of local, gray cut stone stands on a knoll overlooking Strangford Lough, one mile east of

84

the main house. The first-floor room, designed by Stuart, has fine plaster-work and inlaid floors. The decoration is mentioned in Lewis's *Topographical Dictionary* of 1837: "The floors, which are of bog fir, found in the peat moss on the estate, are, for beauty and elegance of design, unequalled by anything in the country."

There is a scullery and wine cellar at basement level, connected by means of an underground passage to a small set of utility rooms where the meals brought from the main house could be kept warm (or cool) by the servants, out of sight of the diners.

In 1786, the plight of the Marquess's son—who was returning home in the midst of a violent storm on the lough—was observed from an upper window of the Temple, and he was rescued. It is interesting to note that the 3rd Marquess, upon the death of his father, flatly rejected the idea "for Turning a Temple built for Mirth & Jollity into a Sepulchre. The place is solely appropriate for a Junketting Retreat in the Grounds."

Since the Temple of the Winds was given to the National Trust in 1982 there has been extensive restoration, and it has been carefully redecorated; the colors for the interiors were chosen by the late John Fowler. The Temple is open to the public during the summer months.

ORLEANS HOUSE

Middlesex, England

The Octagon

86 87 88

Orleans House, Twickenham, was built in 1710 for James Johnston, Joint Secretary of State for Scotland under William III. Its most celebrated occupant, however, was Louis Phillipe, Duc d'Orléans, who lived there during his exile from France (1815–17).

The Octagon was designed by James Gibbs around 1720. It was attached to the end of the house (which has since been pulled down) as a garden pavilion. Built of stone, as well as yellow and red brick, it has the tall, rusticated windows that are a feature of James Gibbs's highly individual style. The domed interior of the Octagon is decorated with exuberant Italianate plasterwork attributed to Artari and Bagutti—who also collaborated on the glorious interior of St. Martin-in-the-Fields.

Orleans House is now a library and gallery owned by the Borough of Richmond, and is open to the public.

87

88

OSTERLEY PARK

Middlesex, England

The Garden House

89   90

The Temple of Pan

91

Osterley Park was totally renovated by Robert Adam in the 1760s—some ten years later he designed the semicircular Garden House. A visitor in 1772 mentioned that "the park is very fine considering it is flat," and John Adams (during a visit to Osterley with Thomas Jefferson) noted in his diary that "The Verdure is charming, the Music of the Birds pleasant."

89

90

The Doric Temple of Pan, also in the "flat" gardens, is said to have been built by John James of Greenwich in 1720, although the plasterwork of the interior would seem to indicate a later date. Originally furnished with a mahogany table and chairs for dining, the Temple may actually have been the work of Sir William Chambers, who was active at Osterley in the 1750s.

Administered by the Victoria and Albert Museum, Osterley Park is a property of the National Trust, and is open to the public.

PITCHFORD HALL

Shropshire, England

The Tree House
92 93 94

The garden of Pitchford Hall is home to a Jacobean Tree House, thought to be the only survivor of its kind in the British Isles. Although it appears to perch on a stout limb of a venerable lime tree, it has recently been reinforced (and thus gained a new lease on life) by having a steel frame fitted beneath it, within the hollow trunk of the tree.

The interior of the Tree House dates from the late eighteenth century, at which time the Gothick ogee windows were installed and the playful, beribboned plasterwork was executed. On a visit to Pitchford Hall in 1832, the thirteen-year-old future Queen Victoria noted in her diary: "We arrived at Pitchford, a curious but very comfortable house. It is striped black-and-white and in the shape of a cottage. At a little past one we walked about the grounds. I went up a staircase to a little house in a tree."

Pitchford Hall is a private residence. Visits to the Tree House are by appointment only.

93

94

RENDLESHAM HALL

Suffolk, England

Woodbridge Lodge

95

Woodbridge Lodge is a simple, one-storied gate lodge at heart, although outwardly it may appear to be in the throes of becoming a cathedral. Built in the late eighteenth century, this architectural extravaganza might have been designed by Henry Hakewill, who gothicized Rendlesham Hall for Peter Isaac Thellusson, the 1st Baron Rendlesham, in 1801. Five heavy flying buttresses soar up over the modest living quarters and join to form a chimney.

Woodbridge Lodge is a private residence.

96

RIEVAULX TERRACE

North Yorkshire, England

The Ionic Temple

96 97 98

Rievaulx Terrace is a superb, half-mile sweep of greensward on a ridge above the picturesque ruins of the celebrated Cistercian Abbey. The farthest points on the Terrace, which was created as part of Duncombe Park, are marked by two garden pavilions—one an Ionic Temple, the other a Doric Temple.

The Ionic Temple was built around 1758 as a banqueting house, and has a painted ceiling by Giovanni Borgnis (who also worked at West Wycombe), based upon celebrated Roman ceilings in the Casino Rospigliosi (*Aurora* by Guido Reni), and in the Palazzo Farnese (mythological scenes by the Carracci). The furnishings of the Temple include a pair of heavily-carved giltwood settees designed by William Kent.

Rievaulx Terrace is a property of the National Trust, and is open to the public.

98

96 ·

97

RUSHTON HALL

Northamptonshire, England

The Triangular Lodge

99 100 101

The Triangular Lodge was built in 1597 by Sir Thomas Tresham, an ardent Roman Catholic in an age when the level of religious tolerance was not high. He built the Triangular Lodge (based on the symbol of the Trinity) more as a monument to his religious obsession than as a useful piece of architecture. In 1581, Tresham had been arrested for hiding the Jesuit Edmund Campion, and was imprisoned for seven years. It is said that, while in prison, he elaborated the complicated iconography of the Lodge.

99

Rushton Hall • continued

The building is three-sided, each side measuring thirty-three feet. It has three stories, three gables on each side, and a total of nine gargoyles. The exterior is littered with trefoils of different dimensions, and the interior has triangular windows. The insistent use of the triangle, of course, is also a pun on the first three letters of Tresham's name.

This defiant statement of religious belief is now in the care of the Department of the Environment, and is open to the public.

100

101

SALTRAM

Devon, England

The Castle

102   103

Saltram is one of the largest and most perfectly preserved eighteenth-century country houses in Devon. Robert Adam worked here extensively in the 1770s. The site, on an estuary surrounded by hills, is one of the loveliest in the country.

There are numerous garden buildings in the park at Saltram—the most substantial being the small, castellated octagon known as the Castle. It was probably designed by Thomas Robinson, later Lord Grantham. The interior, in the style of Adam, is the work of Henry Stockman. The Castle was often used for dining in fine weather.

Saltram is a property of the National Trust, and is open to the public.

102

103

SHERBORNE HOUSE

Gloucestershire, England

Lodge Park
104

The design of Lodge Park, one of the most perfect small houses in England, has been ascribed to Inigo Jones; Lord Burlington was so intrigued by this idea (possibly conveyed to him by William Kent), that he commissioned Harry Flitcroft to make a drawing of the building, which is now in the collection of the Royal Institute of British Architects. It is easy to understand the attribution—from a distance, Lodge Park bears a certain resemblance to Jones's Whitehall Banqueting House in outline and fenestration. (Actually, the design was probably the work of John Webb, Inigo Jones's chief pupil and assistant, but carried out with some variations by the Gloucestershire master-mason, Valentine Strong.)

The Lodge was built for John Dutton in the latter half of the seventeenth century, as a viewing-place or grandstand for deer-coursing. Originally, it had only one large room on each floor, and all were heated by imposing fireplaces. From the roof, there are splendid views over the surrounding countryside.

The Sherborne estate has recently been acquired by the National Trust, and Lodge Park will be open to the public after restoration.

STOURHEAD

Wiltshire, England

105

106

Stourhead is the greatest of the English romantic landscape gardens. It evolved slowly, over a thirty-year period, as the creation of an inspired amateur, Henry Hoare II. Barbara Jones has aptly described it as "achieving a balance between intimacy and space so just that one wonders if serenity may have a mathematical constant."

The Grotto was built in 1748, possibly to Hoare's own designs, with a circular, domed chamber, and a white marble nymph asleep in an alcove over a cascade. Another room in the Grotto forms the Cave of the River God, where a statue of Tiber by Cheere points the way to daylight.

The Pantheon or Temple of Hercules was built in 1754–56 to designs by Harry Flitcroft. It is a domed rotunda with a recessed portico, and within is a statue of Hercules by Rysbrack.

Stourhead · continued

Flitcroft's Temple of Apollo or Temple of the Sun was built around 1765 and is based upon a ruin at Baalbek. It stands on a hill overlooking a vista that Horace Walpole described as being "one of the most picturesque scenes in the world."

107

108

King Alfred's Tower, also designed by Flitcroft in 1765, but not completed until 1772, is one of the tallest folly towers in the British Isles—its triangular and windowless expanse, 160 feet high, was intended for no other purpose than the view it afforded from the top. It is said that Henry Hoare had wanted to replicate the campanile of St. Mark's in Venice, but changed his mind upon reading of the exploits of King Alfred.

Stourhead House and its landscape garden are the property of the National Trust, and they are open to the public.

109

STUDLEY ROYAL

North Yorkshire, England

The gardens of Studley Royal were laid out by John Aislabie, Chancellor of the Exchequer (1714–18), whose political career was destroyed by the scandalous financial collapse that followed the South Sea Bubble swindle in 1720. Aislabie retired to his Yorkshire estate and, together with his son William and their chief gardeners, William Fisher, John Simpson, and Robert Doe, made use of the undulating valley of the river Skell to compose a linked series of gardens with picturesque views and decorative pavilions leading progressively to the genuine ruins of Fountains Abbey.

The so-called Moon Ponds were formed by channeling the river into round and crescent shapes, and it was here that Aislabie built the Temple of Piety around 1728, possibly to his own design. Reflected—together with its thick backdrop of trees—in the ponds' still surfaces, the Temple serves both as eye-catcher and viewpoint.

110

111

The Gothic Tower was originally a classical pavilion that was altered in 1738 by William Aislabie, and transformed into a Gothick belvedere entered from a tunnel in the steep bankside.

The Cascade Houses or Fishing Pavilions were built in 1727, at either end of the dam on the river Skell that effectively transforms the narrow valley into a series of water-parterres. On the western side of the valley, opposite the Moon Ponds, in a clearing with a sunken or "coffin" lawn used as a bowling green, stands Colen Campbell's Banqueting House, built around 1728 and originally an orangery. The strong design makes use of vermiculated rustication in bands, pilasters dripping with stony hoarfrost, balustrades, and sylvan masks.

The noble ruin of the Cistercian Abbey of Fountains forms the culminating "view" and constitutes the grandest eye-catcher in any eighteenth-century garden. It was not purchased until fifty years after John Aislabie had made it the climax of his series of landscape vistas. Founded in the twelfth century, the Abbey flourished until the dissolution of the religious orders by Henry VIII in the sixteenth century.

112

113

In 1983, the National Trust acquired the gardens of Studley Royal, and their long-term conservation is being carefully considered. In *Country Life* (March 27, 1986), Richard Haslam wrote: "The continuing existence of landscape gardens depends not only on the lives of trees and the operating of hydraulics, but on the original ideas remaining clear and attractive over long stretches of time in the minds of those who look after them. It might seem strange that one of the most celebrated works in this branch of art should qualify for that sort of comment; but the fact is that the origins of Studley Royal, despite exhaustive research, remain tantalizingly vague. In piloting it towards its fourth century, the National Trust has had to fall back on the garden itself as its own best document."

Studley Royal Gardens and Fountains Abbey are open to the public.

SWARKESTON

Derbyshire, England

The Stand

114

The Stand was built in 1630–32 by the stonemason Richard Shepherd, for Sir John Harpur of Swarkeston Hall. Its design has been attributed to Robert Smythson. The name implies that it was used as a position from which deer were slaughtered, after having been driven into the forecourt. The stonemason's bill describes it as a "Bowl-alley House," and it may have served a variety of uses—although all of them would have been pastimes, since the building was little more than a belvedere.

The Stand has been acquired by the Landmark Trust, and will be available for short-term holiday rentals.

SYON PARK

Isleworth, Middlesex, England

The Pavilion

115   116   117

The Pavilion, or fishing lodge, idyllically situated on a bend of the Thames in Syon Park, was built in 1802–08 by Robert Mylne for the 2nd Duke of Northumberland, as a present for his wife.

Originally, the Pavilion consisted of a lofty, domed, circular room flanked by a pair of smaller rooms. Three arched windows open onto a narrow, colonnaded balcony that overlooks Kew Gardens across the river. In the boathouse, at river level, the barge that conveyed Lady Jane Grey to her beheading in the Tower of London was stored until as late as 1919. The boathouse was filled in when the Pavilion was enlarged and converted into a gracious and comfortable dwelling.

Syon House, a residence of the Duke of Northumberland, is open to the public. The Pavilion may be viewed from the opposite bank of the Thames.

115

116

117

TENDRING HALL

Suffolk, England

The Fishing Temple

118   119

Sir John Soane built Tendring Hall in 1784–86 for Admiral Rowley. The house was demolished in the 1950s and all that remains is the earlier Georgian fishing lodge attributed to Sir Robert Taylor, whose own house in Richmond it resembles.

The Fishing Temple, or lodge, stands at the short end of a rectangular canal that was formerly stocked with trout. The design is derived from Palladio's Venetian churches, in which a central, pedimented block pushes up through—and separates—a lower one.

Tendring Hall · continued

The interior consists of one large, light, main room (with eighteenth-century plasterwork), over a vaulted undercroft. The fireplace in the main room has an imposing overmantel, and the door seems to have been deliberately set low to accentuate the height of the room.

The Fishing Temple is privately owned.

WARDOUR OLD CASTLE

Wiltshire, England

The Gothic Banqueting House
120   121

The late Georgian Banqueting House perched on the wall of Wardour Old Castle has a Gothick interior, and entrances at both the upper Castle level and the lower lakeside.

Both the Old Castle and the Gothic Banqueting House are in the care of the Department of the Environment, and they are open to the public.

120

121

WESTBURY COURT GARDEN

Gloucestershire, England

The Tall Pavilion
122

Maynard Colchester inherited Westbury Court from his grandfather in 1694, and he must have begun remodeling the garden at once, since it appears in so finished a state in Kip's engraving of 1705. The design makes extensive use of canals, as well as clipped hedges, and has a formal geometric plan, all characteristics of seventeenth-century Dutch gardens. The neighboring family at Flaxley Abbey had connections with Holland, and there seems to have been considerable Dutch influence in the area at the time (see Alkerton Grange and Frampton Court).

Given the horizontality of Dutch gardens, some raised vantage point was needed if the owner was to be able to survey his accomplishment in comfort. This purpose was served by summerhouses, tea-houses, gazebos, and pavilions, many of which can still be seen in the Netherlands. The Tall Pavilion is a survivor of this type of summerhouse; its single room is supported on a loggia of six Ionic columns and surmounted by a pediment, a pitched roof, and a square, windowed lantern. Colchester was a Commissioner of the Forest of Dean and could see the forest, as well as a great deal of the surrounding countryside, from the cozy elegance of his wood-paneled retreat. Originally, the Tall Pavilion had a marble fireplace, which was not replaced when it was rebuilt in 1971 by the National Trust. The feeling of the building—with its enormous, many-paned sash windows, and black-and-white paved loggia—is decidedly Dutch.

There is also a small brick gazebo in the gardens, built during the second quarter of the eighteenth century. This building nestles in the corner of a walled garden with a lily pool in which there stands a statue of Neptune. Colchester's accounts for the garden are preserved in the Gloucester Record Office, and are fascinatingly meticulous: on October 5, 1704, he paid "Smart for pineaples and pillers £1:17:4." These are the decorative elements on the two piers that flank the *clairvoyée* set in the wall at the end of the long canal, opposite the summerhouse. A second *clairvoyée* was added after 1715, flanked by elaborate urns.

Westbury Court Garden was acquired by the National Trust in 1967, and is open to the public.

WESTON PARK

Staffordshire, England

The Temple of Diana

123   124   125   126

The Temple of Diana was built in 1770 to designs by James Paine for Sir Henry Bridgeman (no relation to Charles Bridgeman, the pioneering landscape architect who died in 1738), as the centerpiece of a complete landscape garden scheme by Capability Brown. It was conceived as a multiple-use pleasure pavilion with an arcaded orangery on the south front. This resplendent conservatory has a superbly decorated ceiling based upon the then recently-discovered ancient Roman wall decoration at Herculaneum. The harmonious composition consists of an oval supported on a rectangle: the deft transition from one form to the other is effected by curved triangular pendentives that spring from tall Ionic columns.

124

125

126

Behind the orangery, Paine's ingenious design provides an entirely different elevation—a domed, canted bay of two stories, flanked by wings. The central bay contains the circular Tea Room with paintings representing the exploits of Diana. To the left of the Tea Room is the elegant octagonal room known variously as the Music Room, the China Room, or the Blue and White Room; it is fitted with alcoves and standing shelves upon which were formerly arranged china and biscuit wares. On the other side of the circular room is what Paine himself described as "the habitation of a dairy woman" who occupied "an exceeding good bed-chamber under the dome." There is a basement, which contains a vaulted dairy and a gloomy stone bath.

Weston Park is the seat of the Earls of Bradford, and is open to the public.

WEST WYCOMBE PARK

Buckinghamshire, England

The Music Pavilion
127

The Music Pavilion was built for Sir Francis Dashwood in the 1750s by Nicholas Revett, on an island in the lake of West Wycombe Park. West Wycombe Park was the meeting-place of the notorious Hell Fire Club—Sir Francis being one of its founder-members. Although admittedly given to orgies and rites of black magic, the Hell Fire Club may have used the chaste island temple for less strenuous revels.

Sir Francis Dashwood commissioned Revett "to execute various architectural works in the Greek gusto." The cascade, designed in 1761, is adorned with statues of sleeping nymphs by Michael Rysbrack, based on antique originals in the Capitoline Museum in Rome. The Pavilion, as its name implies, was used for musical performances, and also for theatrical representations. Its design owes something to the Temple of Vesta in Rome. The interior has luminous frescoes by Giovanni Borgnis, based on those by the Carracci in the Palazzo Farnese in Rome. This Italian artist was brought to England by Sir Francis Dashwood in 1751 to work at West Wycombe (his painted ceilings can also be seen in the Ionic Temple at Rievaulx).

Although it continues to be the home of the Dashwood family, West Wycombe and its landscape garden are the property of the National Trust, and both are open to the public.

127

WILTON HOUSE

Wiltshire, England

The Palladian Bridge at Wilton was built in 1737 by the 9th Earl of Pembroke, sometimes known as the "Architect Earl," and Roger Morris. The Bridge is a successful reduction of Palladio's design for the Rialto Bridge, published in the *Quattro Libri*. This design was so popular that it was copied at both Prior Park and Stowe.

The Old Schoolhouse was built in 1838, using the facade of the seventeenth-century grotto designed by Isaac de Caus for the Caroline garden at Wilton. The grotto stood at the end of the Great Walk, facing the garden front of the house, and—to judge by contemporary accounts—had hidden jets that could be turned on to "wash the spectator for a diversion." The elaborate carvings of putti, faces, and foliage are executed in soft limestone "recalling the effect of such provincial Baroque decoration as is found in Lecce or in Mexican churches." The work was probably executed by Nicolas Stone the younger, who was responsible for the sumptuous carving in the famous Double Cube Room in Wilton House. In 1838, the carvings from the front of the grotto were reassembled by James Wyatt and used as a facade for the Old Schoolhouse.

129

130

Wilton House · continued

The Casino (or *Casina*), which sits on a hillside opposite the house, was designed by Sir William Chambers for the 10th Earl, and built in the 1750s of exquisitely-cut Chilmark stone. It appears in Chambers's *Treatise* of 1791, and is described as "having been built some years ago at Wilton. . . . It consists of a small salon and portico above, and of a little kitchen or servants' waiting room below." Access to the "salon" is via two lateral outside staircases to the balustraded loggia.

The Holbein Porch is a piece of the original sixteenth-century house, whose design was traditionally attributed to the painter Holbein. Around 1805, this porch was placed in its present position at the end of a garden walk by James Wyatt.

Wilton House is the seat of the Earls of Pembroke, and is open to the public.

131

132

WOBURN ABBEY

Bedfordshire, England

The Chinese Dairy

133 134

The Thornery

135 136

The great park of Woburn Abbey has a large assortment of delightful garden conceits: a Chinese temple, a grotto of 1630 by Isaac de Caus, a circular, domed icehouse by Henry Holland, and even a mock Tudor house from the 1878 Paris Exhibition. But the two outstanding follies are the Chinese Dairy and the Thornery.

The Chinese Dairy at Woburn was built in the 1790s by Henry Holland for the 5th Duke of Bedford, during the period that Holland was at work on Woburn Abbey itself. At first glance, the Dairy might seem a considerable digression from Holland's usual cool Neoclassicism, but beyond its chinoiserie, the elevation is not far from the blocks with cupolas and temple-fronts that Holland was designing in London.

Set on a lake close to the house, the Dairy has a long, curved arcade probably meant for strolling in wet weather. The interior has a complex, faceted ceiling painted with fretwork.

There are niches with fretwork shelves, as well as gilded and delicately carved wall brackets meant to hold the "profusion of white marble and coloured glasses . . . hundreds of large dishes and bowls of Chinese and Japanese porcelain . . . filled with new milk and cream" noted by a nineteenth-century visitor. The windows have painted glass by J. T. Perrache, dated 1794 and 1795.

The Thornery, Humphry Repton's rustic retreat of 1806, is a fairy-tale thatched summerhouse in a clearing in the woods on the estate. It is square in plan, with four gables. The interior, presently undergoing extensive repair and restoration, is playful and eccentric—as befits a building that was used only occasionally,

134

135

and then principally for bucolic luncheons. The ceiling (as in the Chinese Dairy) is complex, and painted with *trompe l'oeil* trellis. A round window is set over the fireplace and, another sophisticated pleasantry, there is a convex mirror set into the wall that reflects a droll, distorted picture of the entire room. At a little distance down the hillside, out of sight of the Thornery, is a pretty tiled kitchen with stained-glass windows. A simple set of Wedgwood china was made especially for the Thornery. The cost of construction and furnishings was £ 700.

Woburn Abbey is the home of the Russell family, Dukes of Bedford, and is open to the public.

136

WREST PARK

Bedfordshire, England

Thomas Archer (1668–1743) was one of the few architects of the English Baroque whose work shows the influence of Borromini. The Pavilion or banqueting house he built in 1711 for the Duke of Kent at Wrest is based on that Italian architect's *S. Ivo alla Sapienza* in Rome. Sir John Summerson has remarked that, not long after this date, "Borromini—the *enfant terrible* of Italian architecture" was to be regarded "much as a good schoolboy regards a prostitute"—an attitude that persisted well into the present century, one might add.

Built of brick and stone, the domed Pavilion stands at the end of an ornamental canal preceded by a statue of William III by Andrew Carpentière.

137

Wrest Park • continued

The interior walls and ceilings are decorated with illusionistic painting by the Huguenot artist Mark Anthony Hauduroy, dated 1712. The basement contained a kitchen, and rooms for domestic use, reached by twin spiral stairs (presumably to facilitate up-and-down traffic while meals were being served) concealed in the thickness of the walls in the main body of the building. There is a servant's room in the dome, also reached by ingeniously concealed stairs in apse-like projections. However, the ubiquitous Horace Walpole was not impressed—he found the gardens "very ugly in the old-fashioned manner with high hedges and canals, at the end of the principal one of which is a frightful temple by Mr. Archer."

138

139

The Bowling Green House was built around 1740, and is thought to be the work of Batty Langley. It is a long, low rectangle with an Ionic portico and diminutive wings. The single large room is sumptuously decorated in the style of William Kent, with a carved wooden chimneypiece bearing the arms of Henry de Grey, Duke of Kent. The building served as a banqueting house, and has recently been restored.

Wrest Park is in the care of the Department of the Environment, and is open to the public.

141

140

BIBLIOGRAPHY

Headley, Gwyn, and Meulankamp, Wim, *Follies: A National Trust Guide*, London, 1986

Jellicoe, Goode and Lancaster, eds., *The Oxford Companion to Gardens*, London, 1986

Jones, Barbara, *Follies & Grottoes* (rev. ed.), London, 1974

Mowl, Tim, and Earnshaw, Brian, *Trumpet at a Distant Gate: The Lodge as Prelude to the Country House*, London, 1985

Pevsner, Nikolaus, *The Buildings of England* Series

Rowan, Alistair, *Garden Buildings*, Feltham, 1968

Smith, John, ed., *The Landmark Handbook*, Shottesbrooke, 1977

Summerson, Sir John, *Architecture in Britain 1530–1850*, London, 1970

INDEX

ACKNOWLEDGMENTS

We wish to thank the following for their advice, help, and hospitality: Christian Aall, the Duke of Beaufort, Mrs. Beaumont, Charles Beresford-Clark, Sir William and Lady Boulton, the Earl of Bradford, the Duke of Buccleuch and Queensberry, the Lord Burnham, Alfred Bush, Viscountess Campden, the Dowager Marchioness of Cholmondeley, Mr. & Mrs. Oliver Colthurst, Mr. & Mrs. Dawes, Austin Dunphy, Mr. & Mrs. George Lane Fox, the Earl of Gainsborough, Mr. & Mrs. Hall, Charlotte Haslam, John Harris, Neville Hawkes, William Hawkes, Mr. & Mrs. G. Holbech, Mrs. Hurlock, Gervase Jackson-Stops, Lady Victoria Leatham, Alison McVeigh, Sean and Rosemarie Mulcahy, Robert Nicholls, the Duke of Northumberland, the Earl of Pembroke, Lady Maria Pridden, the Duke of Richmond, John Smith, John Saumarez Smith, the Viscount Scarsdale, the Earl of Shelburne, the Hon. Guy R. Strutt, the Marquess of Tavistock, Mr. Thompson, Lavinia Wellicome, Roger White, Andrew Williams, the Earl of Yarborough, the Marquess of Zetland. We also thank the National Trust, the Department of the Environment, the Commissioners of Public Works, Dublin, and the Landmark Trust, for allowing us access to properties in their expert care.

A special word of thanks and appreciation is due to the designer, Paul Steinberg, who helped with the photography.

George Mott and Sally Sample Aall
New York 1988